PUB WALKS
IN CORNWALL

Forty Circular Walks

Around Cornwall Inns

David Hancock

Other Publications in the series.
"Pub Walks in Dorset".
"Forty More Pub Walks in Dorset".
"Pub Walks in Hampshire and the I.O.W."
"Pub Walks in West Sussex".
"Pub Walks in Devon".

Planned for 1994
"Pub Walks in Somerset".
"Pub Walks in Kent".

1st edition published May 1993.

Acknowledgements
In researching this book I am indebted to the contribution of my friend and colleague Bonita Toms who accompanied me on all the walks. Bonita took all the photographs and made many invaluable observations and notes on each walk. I would also like to thank all the landlords for their help and enthusiasm in the idea of pub walks.

Publisher's Note
Whilst every care has been taken to ensure that all the information given in this book is correct, errors will occur due to many factors. Paths can be re-routed, stiles can replace gates, etc. and the pub themselves often change hands. Neither the publishers nor the printers can accept responsibility for any inaccuracies.

Power Publications
1, Clayford Ave
Ferndown
Dorset. BH22 9PQ

STD PHONE NUMBERS
All phone numbers in the area covered by this publication need the figure 1 inserted after the initial zero. For example, 0556 (the code for Altarnum) becomes 01556.

Printed by Pardy & Son (Printers) Ltd, Ringwood, Hants.

Front cover: Shipwrights Arms, Helford.

INTRODUCTION

Cornwall's long rugged peninsula is characterised by its striking coastal scenery, much of it deeply indented by wide river estuaries and dotted with picturesque fishing coves and villages, steeped in smuggling and wrecking history. The windswept interior gives way to open moorland, rich in industrial and archeological treasures. The 40 walks included here seek to explore some of the beauty and legends that this county has to offer.

Although Cornwall has for many years been a mecca for tourists, suffering its fair share of commercialism, there are still plenty of unspoilt stretches of coastline and small villages that harbour delightful traditional hostelries, all serving real ale. After touring the whole county in search of Cornwall's best pubs, the selection included have been chosen either for their charm and character or their splendid coastal location and vicinity to interesting walks. No charge has been made for the pub's inclusion in this book.

The walks are all circular, ranging between $2\frac{1}{2}$ miles to $6\frac{1}{2}$ miles in length and as well as a detailed route description and sketch map, there are pointers to places of interest on route. The walks are fairly short in order to appeal to families and are planned to start and finish at the pub, although it is possible start anywhere along the route. If you are planning to use the pub it is only courteous to ask the landlord's permission first.

In general footpaths in Cornwall are well marked, this is especially the case along the 268 miles of coast path – much of it National Trust land – and within the immediate vicinity inland. Further inland many of the paths, although way-marked from roads, are ill-defined and awkward to follow. Where parish councils have produced leaflets on local walks the paths are well signposted. To help you the reference quoted at the start of each walk refers to the 1:50 000 $1\frac{1}{4}$ inch to the mile in the Landranger series. The five maps you would need to cover the whole county are nos. 190, 200, 201, 203 and 204. There are more detailed maps in the Pathfinder series which cover an area 1:25 000 – $2\frac{1}{2}$ inches to the mile.

The new "Rights of Way" Act, which came into force on August 13th, 1990, has much improved the rights of ramblers; it is a massive step forward in path protection. The Act now requires occupiers who disturb the land to make good the surface within 24 hours of the disturbance or two weeks if the disturbance is the first one for a particular crop. Where no width is recorded the minimum width of a path must be apparent on the ground. If you find a footpath blocked the law allows for you to remove only as much of the obstruction to get by, but not to cause damage. If there is now way through you have the right to leave the path and find an alternative route. Any problems you find should be reported to the county engineer in the Countryside Access section of the County Council at Radnor Road, Scorrier, Redruth.

On all these walks it is advisable to wear suitable clothing and to take light weight waterproof trousers or leggings, as many paths become overgrown in the summer. A waterproof jacket or cagoule is an essential item as many of the walks cross windy exposed cliffs and a sudden shower is not uncommon. Strong waterproof boots are best but any comfortable footwear will do provided it is well treaded.

Take care on lanes without pavements and always walk facing the oncoming traffic, except on a dangerous right hand bend. A compass can be useful when traversing open moorland and a torch is handy if walking late in the evening.

Wherever you go always remember the country code. Guard against all fires. Fasten gates. Keep dogs under control and always on a lead where there are livestock. Keep to the path across farmland. Take all litter home. Respect wildlife and do not pick flowers. We hope you enjoy these walks and the hospitality and individual charm of all the pubs as much as we did during our research.

David Hancock

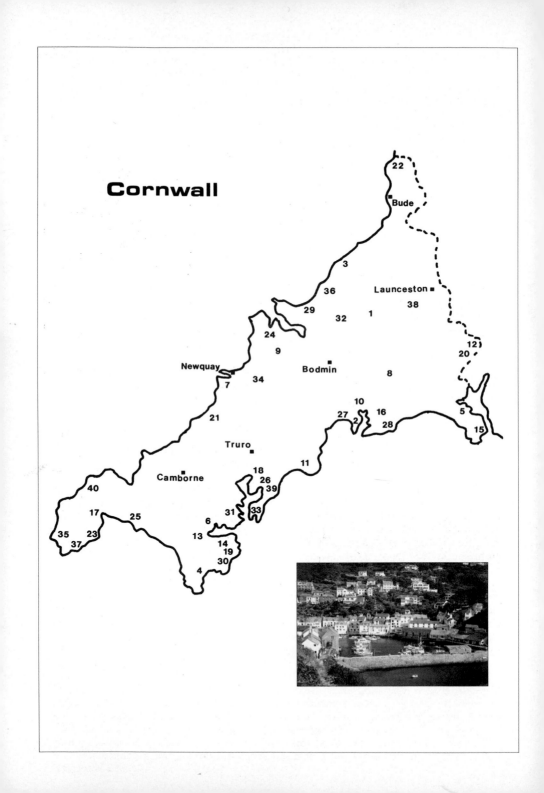

Cornwall

22

■Bude

3

36
Launceston ■
38
29
32   1

24
9

Newquay ■   Bodmin ■   8
7   34

12
20

21
10
27   16
2   28
5
15

Truro ■   11

18
Camborne ■   26
39
40
31   33
17   25   6
35   23   13
37   14
19
30
4

Walk	Town/Village	Miles	Inn	Page
1	Altarnun	5½	The Rising Sun	6
2	Bodinnick	4	The Old Ferry Inn	9
3	Boscastle	3½	Napoleon Inn	11
4	Cadgwith Cove	3½	Cadgwith Cove Inn	14
5	Cargreen	3½	The Spaniards Inn	16
6	Constantine	4	Trengilly Wartha Inn	18
7	Crantock	5	The Old Albion	20
8	Crows Nest	3½	Crows Nest Inn	22
9	Egloshayle	6	The Earl of St. Vincent	24
10	Golant	3	Fishermans Arms	26
11	Gorran Churchtown	5½	The Barley Sheaf	28
12	Gunnislake	3½	The Rising Sun	30
13	Gweek	3	The Black Swan	32
14	Helford	2¾	Shipwrights Arms	34
15	Kingsand	6	The Halfway House Inn	36
16	Lerryn	5	The Ship	38
17	Ludgvan	3½	The White Hart	42
18	Malpas	3½	The Heron Inn	44
19	Manaccan	5	New Inn	46
20	Metherell	4½	The Carpenters Arms	49
21	Mithian	4½	The Miners Arms	52
22	Morwenstow	4½	The Bush Inn	54
23	Mousehole	4	The Ship Inn	58
24	Padstow	5	The Shipwrights	60
25	Perranuthnoe	4½	The Victoria Inn	62
26	Philleigh	6	Roseland Inn	65
27	Polkerris	3½	The Rashleigh Inn	68
28	Polperro	4½	The Blue Peter Inn	70
29	Port Gaverne	3½	Port Gaverne Hotel	72
30	Porthallow	4	Five Pilchards Inn	74
31	Restronguet Creek	5	The Pandora Inn	76
32	St. Breward	2½	The Old Inn	78
33	St. Mawes	5½	The Rising Sun	80
34	St. Mawgan	6¾	The Falcon Inn	82
35	Sennen Cove	4½	Old Success Inn	84
36	Trebarwith Strand	3¾	The Port William	86
37	Treen	3	The Logan Rock Inn	88
38	Tregadillett	3½	The Eliot Arms	91
39	Veryan	4½	New Inn	93
40	Zennor	4½	The Tinners Arms	95

The Rising Sun, Altarnun

The 16th century Rising Sun was originally a farmhouse operating 30 acres. It gained its first license in 1846, yet remained a farm and ale house until 40 years ago, when most of the land was sold. It enjoys an unspoilt and remote rural setting on the fringe of Bodmin Moor and was a popular trading post for market traders carrying their produce by cart to the major markets. The rather run-down exterior appearance belies the true rustic and lively atmosphere that fills the distinctive beamed bar. Traditional wood and slate floors are lined with sturdy tables, stools and padded wall bench seating and a stone fireplace with open log fire warms the bar. Beyond this bar area there are two further simple rooms, one with a pool table, the other being a family room.

The inn is a free house in the capable hands of the owner Les Humphreys who is keen on dispensing a wide range of real ales, especially unusual brews from small breweries. On my winter visit Cotleigh Tawny, Morland Original and the regular beer Flowers Original were on offer. In summer months the range increases to at least five ales.

A comprehensive range of bar food is served from 12 noon till 2.30 p.m. and 6.30 p.m. till 9.45 p.m. Hearty snacks include home-made soup, pasty, cauliflower cheese, cottage pie, ploughmans sandwiches and a choice of jacket potatoes with fillings. The main menu features a selection of hot dishes such as cannelloni, vegetable chilli, various omelettes, moussaka, rump steak and meat pie, all served with a salad garnish. Excellent blackboard specials – seafood pie, Italian chicken, lamb casserole or beef in Guinness – supplement the printed menu. A couple of puddings are available, usually a home-made fruit pie or a sponge served with custard. The roast Sunday lunch is good, very popular and superb value-for-money. Children have their own menu.

Weekday opening times are from 11 a.m. till 3 p.m. and 5.30 p.m. till 11 p.m.

Children are welcome in the family room and dogs are most welcome in the bar.

The inn offers overnight accommodation in four bedrooms and camping is available in the field opposite.

Telephone: (0556) 86636.

Altarnun lies off the A30. The pub is situated 1 mile north of the village on the Five Lanes to Camelford road and is well signposted.

Approx. distance of walk: 5½ miles. O.S. Map No. 201 SX 215/825.

The inn has a large car park opposite.

This is a peaceful undulating ramble across delightful scenic field paths through the parish of Altarnun – the largest parish in Cornwall. The landscape views are dominated by the northern edge of Bodmin Moor and the walk also allows the opportunity to visit Wesley Cottage, where the Methodist preacher John Wesley stayed when he visited the area. Good stout footware is necessary, as it can be extremely wet and muddy underfoot.

1. From the car park turn left along the narrow lane and keep ahead on reaching a crossroads, towards South Carne. Shortly, cross a river bridge and bear left uphill for South Carne. At the top of the rise, where the lane bears right, turn left onto a way-marked footpath towards Tresmeake Farm. Follow the concrete drive through the farmyard to a gate and proceed ahead along a wide muddy track to two gates. Go through the left hand gate, keep to the right hand edge and soon pass through two gaps into further pastures. In the third field bear half-left to a metal gate and small brook. Beyond the gate, head straight up the centre of the field ahead, with a farm to your left. Pass through a gate and turn left along a lane towards the farm.

2. At a left hand bend, bear right at the footpath sign and pass in front of the farm, along a track to a gate. Proceed ahead along the old banked trackway, following it gently downhill into a field. A yellow arrow directs you left along a track, across a brook, then just before you reach a gate, keep ahead through scrub to a stile. Keep to the left of a boggy area and cross a footbridge to a stile. Bear half-right across the field to another stile over a wall, then gradually climb uphill along the right hand edge of the field, with good views across Altarnun church to your left. Cross a wall stile and from here follow the well waymarked route across pasture, over three stiles and through three gates before bearing left along a lane to the old A30 at Trewint. If wishing to visit Wesleys Cottage turn right, then first left along Duck Street.

3. The main route bears left along the old A30 (pavement), round a right hand bend and just beyond a house called Newchalls, turn left onto a signed path towards Altarnun. Follow the left hand edge of the field down to a stile and join a narrow banked path that takes you across a further stile and through two kissing gates to a lane.

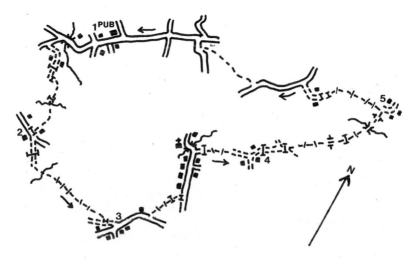

Turn left and enter the picturesque village of Altarnun, with its fine 15th century pack-horse bridge and impressive church, known as the "Cathedral of the Moors". On reaching the Post Office, take the waymarked path right towards Tresmaine and pass through a gate into a barnyard. Cross a stile, head uphill across pasture to a granite stile in the hedge, then bear half-left uphill to a fieldgate. Good views back over the village. Follow the left hand hedgerow to a second gate and stile and shortly enter Tresmaine farm.

4. Bear left onto a concrete drive, your route is signed to Oldhay and Trenarrett and soon swings right to a gate, then onto a green lane. Where this veers sharp left, keep ahead through a gate into pasture and bear half-left to follow the path gently downhill to a wall stile in the corner. Proceed left handed along the edge of a field to a further stile and bear slightly left over the next field through a gap in the hedge, then bear left downhill to a small gate. Keep ahead, then along the left hand hedge, through an old gateway to two gates. Pass through the gate on the left and head downhill, around Old-

hay farm, then proceed steeply downhill into the river valley. Cross a wall stile, head across pasture to a footbridge over Penpont Water and head uphill on a defined path through a gateway to reach Tresnarrett farm.

5. On reaching the field corner, just before the farm, turn left along the field edge (arrow) to a stile in the corner. Keep ahead to a wall stile beside a telegraph pole, then proceed across pasture to a stile slightly obscured in the hedgerow. Go over a small brook and keep straight on uphill. Shortly, Trebullom farm comes into view and soon cross the stile beside a pole fence. Pass round to the right of a small barn, then bear left to pass through two gates into the farmyard. Go through a further two gates and follow the driveway out to a lane. Turn left and follow the narrow lane to where it veers round to the left. Turn right here onto an old sunken track. This soon narrows to a defined hedged path which eventually emerges out to a lane. Turn right, then left at the T-junction and follow the lane for $\frac{1}{2}$ mile back to the pub.

Altarnun Church

The Old Ferry Inn, Bodinnick

A ferry has been plying the waters between Fowey and the tiny village of Bodinnick since the 13th century and for 400 years the delightful Old Ferry Inn has provided refreshment for travellers using the ferry. The whitewashed stone inn is set just above the slipway and looks out across the River Fowey to the picturesque town of Fowey. It has a special charm, the friendly traditionally furnished public bar has black painted, half-panelled walls which are hung with seafaring prints and local photographs of bygone days. The family/games room beyond the public bar actually burrows into the rock face. The comfortable lounge area is carpeted and is furnished with a mix of wheel-back and captain's chairs, stools and bench seating around Victorian style round tables. Its walls are adorned with sailing photographs, stuffed fish in glass cases, a magnificent "parliament clock" and many nautical artefacts. There is no outside seating, except for residents and those visiting for morning coffee, which is served in the upstairs lounge and on the adjoining "sun-trap" terrace.

The inn is a free house efficiently run by its owner Simon Farr with a choice of two real ales dispensed by hand pump such as St. Austell Tinners Ale and the stronger and maltier Flowers Original.

Bar food is limited to a few simple and hearty snacks. Choose from home-made soup and roll, quiche and salad, ploughmans, fishermans lunch (mackerel), farmhouse lunch (ham) and from a range of excellent sandwiches. Food can be ordered in the bar between 12 noon till 2 p.m. and from 6 p.m. till 9 p.m. The inn is locally well known for its value-for-money table d'Hote menu served in the comfortable restaurant from 7.30 p.m. each evening (one sitting). The popular window seat has superb views across the river.

Families are welcome, so too are dogs.

Weekday opening times are from 11 a.m. till 3 p.m. and from 6 p.m. till 11 p.m.

The inn has thirteen letting bedrooms.

Telephone: (0726) 870237.

Walk No. 2

Village can be reached from the west by using the ferry from Fowey and from the east it is 5½ miles from the B3359 at Lanreath.

Approx. distance of walk: 4 miles. O.S. Map No. 200 SX 130/522.

The inn has a car park up the hill. It is possible to park on the hill but make sure your handbrake is working well. There is a further parking area (free) along the lane to the left of the ferry.

A magnificent walk with beautiful ever-changing views across the Fowey estuary and down into Pont Pill Creek. Undulating, easy going wooded paths to Polruan, returning via two ferry crossings and a stroll through historic Fowey.

1. Leave the inn and follow the lane uphill to a waymarked path on the right signed "Hall Walk and Polruan 4 miles". Pass between two cottages onto National Trust land following a level, grassy path past the war memorial. Frequent benches encourage the walker to pause a while to savour the excellent views across the Fowey estuary. Pass a plaque in a shelter stating that Hall Walk was where King Charles narrowly escaped death during the Civil War on 17th August 1664. At a further memorial the panorama includes Pont Pill Creek, Polruan, Fowey, the estuary dotted with hundreds of boats and views out to sea.

2. Bear left with the path, high above Pont Pill Creek and keep to this path as it undulates through scrub and woodland with occasional views into the tranquil, heavily wooded creek. Cross a stile, turn right along the edge of a field and soon re-enter a wood via a gate and head gradually downhill. Bear right at a junction of paths signed "Polruan" down towards the creek. Shortly, join a track, cross a wooden footbridge over the river at the head of the creek and proceed ahead following the waymarked path beside Pont Creek Cottage.

3. Turn right up a series of steps to a stile.

Climb this and head uphill, up wooden steps onto a defined path high above the creek. Cross a stile and follow the "Polruan" sign directing the route along a wide trackway through woodland. Eventually emerge from the thick woodland where occasional cameo views can be enjoyed across the estuary and boats to Fowey and begin to descend into the quaint fishing harbour of Polruan. Go down some concrete steps, bear right onto a tarmac path in front of some cottages and remain on this down to the harbour, bearing right by the Harbour Café for the quay.

4. Take the passenger ferry to Fowey which runs every 15 minutes until 10.45 p.m. (40p. adults, 15p. children). From the ferry steps in Fowey head uphill and turn right along the street into the village centre. Remain on the main street to the far end of the village, then bear right down to the ferry landing stage for the crossing back to Bodinnick. In winter months the ferry operates Monday-Friday daylight to dusk, Saturday 8 a.m.-dusk and Sunday 9 a.m.-dusk. In summer. Monday-Saturday 7 a.m.-8.45 p.m. and Sunday 8 a.m.-8.45 p.m. (30p. adults, 15p. children). From the slipway head uphill back to the pub.

The Napoleon Inn, Boscastle

Located high above the picturesque harbour in the old village is the pretty 16th century Napoleon Inn – a name derived from a period when the building was a recruiting station during the Napoleonic wars. Built of solid stone the inn comprises a number of cosy small low-beamed rooms with polished slate floors. The main bar has a large stone fireplace with a winter log fire, an assortment of tables and chairs including an old settle and window bench seat. Large original beams, a few modern ones and rough white painted stone walls help create the rustic traditional ambience. As would be expected there are a few pictures of Napoleon himself dotted around the walls. A separate games room has a dart board and a pool table. Outside there is a sheltered terrace and a large garden with play area and views out to sea.

The pub is a popular free house dispensing excellent Draught Bass and St. Austell Hicks Special straight from the cask and guest beers such as Greene King Abbot Ale and Mitchells ESB by hand pump.

Bar food is served Monday to Saturday from 12 noon till 2.30 p.m. and from 7 p.m. till 9.30 p.m. and on Sundays from 12 till 2 p.m. and till 9 p.m. in the evenings. Good value lunchtime snacks include soup, pasties, curries, ploughmans and salads with a blackboard menu featuring more substantial home-made dishes, available both at lunchtime and in the evening, for example, devilled lamb steak, beef stroganoff, cottage pie, nasi goreng, various steaks and a vegetarian choice – vegetable stir-fry or a curry. The pub is a popular eating destination in the height of the season especially.

Children are welcome in either of the front rooms and dogs are allowed in.

Weekday opening times are from 12 noon till 3 p.m. and from 7 p.m. to 11 p.m. Telephone: (0840) 250204.

Walk No. 3

Boscastle is situated 5 miles north of Camelford on the B3266.

Approx. distance of walk: 3½ miles. O.S. Map No. 190 SX 099/906.

There is a car park at the side of the inn and along the lane.

An undulating ramble encompassing the picturesque natural harbour, the impressive cliff path and field paths affording open views on the return journey.

1. On leaving the pub turn left to the crossroads and go across to follow the narrow village street downhill towards the harbour. Eventually reach the main road at the Wellington Hotel. Taking care on the bend, cross over onto the metalled lane that runs to the left of the River Valency to the harbour. In its heyday, prior the railways reaching Cornwall in 1893, more than a dozen ketches and many schooners traded regularly through the little port, bringing coal, timber, wines and spirits through the tortuous harbour entrance. At the old granite bridge bear left with the coast path sign and yellow arrow up a shingle track behind a white cottage. Bear left again prior a gate to some cottages onto a shaley level path. Soon good views of the harbour entrance and the blowhole – Devil's Bellows – beneath Penally point opposite.

2. Gradually ascend on the narrow coast path and pass through a walk-through stile. A short detour can be made here by turning right up to the lookout tower on top of Willapark (NT) promontory, for some unrivalled coastal views. The main path shortly follows the top of the cliff to the edge of a field. Where the path divides keep right (yellow arrow) and descend slate steps to a stile. Continue on the coast path. Climb another stile and leave NT land. Follow the path round the next headland, drop down some wooden steps into a stream-fed combe. Cross a footbridge and stile, climb out of the combe and bear right with arrow around the edge of grassland. Cross a slate stile – cliff views right, Trevalga church to the left – the pathway shortly merging with a wider grassy track. Pass through a wooden swing gate and leave the coast path. Follow the shaley track into the hamlet of Trevalga.

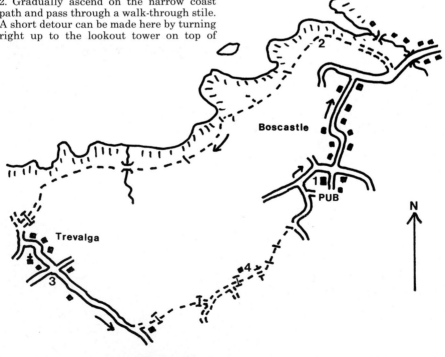

3. Soon merge with a metalled lane, pass the church and continue to the B-road. Go straight across to follow the lane uphill, past the converted chapel to a footpath sign on the left. Keep left of the gates to the Old Rectory, pass through a wooden gate and follow the arrow directing you along the field edge, along the line of telegraph poles. At the end of the wall bear half-right to a gate in the corner, the route being arrowed through Trehane Farm ahead.

4. Beyond the farm bear half-right with arrow and follow the wall. Keep to the edge of the field, through a gap, then an arrow waymarks you diagonally left across a field towards the church in Boscastle. Cross a stone stile into another field and bear half-left downhill on a defined path. Where the path forks keep right to a stile in the hedge (yellow arrow), then follow the path beside a wire fence downhill to a granite stile in the hedge. Climb the stile, turn left onto a lane and follow it downhill to the B-road. Cross over onto the pavement and turn right towards the village. At the sharp left-hand bend cross over onto a lane and follow this back to the pub.

The Picturesque Harbour

Cadgwith Cove Inn, Cadgwith Cove

Cadgwith is a small, picturesque fishing community of pink and whitewashed cottages, once famous for pilchard fishing. The 300 year old smugglers inn overlooks the old pilchard cellar and the steep shingle beach lined with colourful fishing vessels. The inn has remained unchanged since the old smuggling days, the two rustic bars are simply furnished with wall bench seats and chairs around wooden tables. There is a small open fire in each bar. Relics of bygone seafaring days adorn the walls including prints and photographs of old fishermen and scenes of Cadgwith many years ago. The half-wood panelled lounge bar opens out onto a "sun-trap" patio with wooden benches and is floodlit in the summer, making an ideal spot for an evening drink. The inn is popular with visitors and the local fishermen who are renowned locally for their singing, a traditional pastime in the cove.

The inn is a Devenish pub enthusiastically run by Brian and Margaret Chivers and serves on hand pump three traditional real ales, Cornish Original, Flowers IPA and Marstons Pedigree plus Flowers Original straight from the barrel behind the bar.

It is a popular place to eat, the regular bar menu being supplemented by a specials board on which the daily dishes, usually excellent fresh local fish are chalked up. A good choice of sandwiches include local crab, jacket potatoes are generously filled and ploughmans are good value. Hot specials may include monkfish chips and peas and fresh cod and chips. Puddings range from apple pie to fruit crumble. Vegetarians are catered for and children have their own menu. Bar food is served daily from 12 noon till 2 p.m. and from 7 p.m. till 9 p.m. A separate restaurant menu is available between 7 p.m. and 9.30 p.m.

Weekday opening times are from 12 noon till 3 p.m. and 6.30 p.m. till 11 p.m.

Children are welcome in the lounge bar, but after 8 p.m. only over 14's are allowed in. There is no objection to well behaved dogs.

The inn has five letting bedrooms.

Telephone: (0326) 290513.

From Helston follow the signs to The Lizard on the A3083. Cadgwith is signed after 8 miles on the left. Follow the road through Ruan Minor and down into the cove.

Approx. distance of walk: 3½ miles. O.S. Map 203/204 SW 721/145.

Parking is very difficult at the inn and in the cove area. It is best to park in the large public car park behind the village and walk the short distance to the cove.

A spectacular cliff walk along the coast path to picturesque Church Cove, returning to Cadgwith along scenic field paths. Undulating, yet easy going underfoot.

1. From the pub turn right and walk the few yards downhill passing the shingle beach and fishing boats on the left. Proceed uphill out of the cove where at the tight right hand bend bear left onto the signed coast path and follow it gradually uphill with views back over the cove. Join a lane, bear left and follow the sign to the Devils Frying Pan along a tarmac path to the left of a large house. This joins a metalled driveway, follow this uphill and turn left at coast path sign and pass in front of "Town Place". Shortly, enter National Trust land and pass the natural phenomena known as the Devils Frying Pan, an enormous collapsed sea cavern. The well walked path now follows the top of the cliff with fine sea views, the Lizard to the right and Black Head away to the left. The path here is level and narrow and in summer resplendant with wild flowers, especially foxgloves. Remain on this path which enjoys stunning cliff scenery towards Church Cove and the lifeboat station visible ahead. Cross a stile before descending down into the cove.

2. Once in Church Cove bear right onto a stony trackway away from the sea passing a thatched cottage called "The Mariners" before joining a metalled lane which passes through the quaint hamlet to the church. Turn right onto a signed pathway in front of the church wall and follow a fine old cobbled green lane between high hedges to a stone stile. Cross into meadowland and proceed downhill on a defined path bearing left at the bottom after crossing a tiny brook. The path winds through gorse covered scrubland, gradually bearing right uphill. Climb a stile in the corner, keep right along the field edge to another stile and head towards the house ahead. Shortly, cross a wall stile to follow the waymarked route left along a track towards "Trethvas Farm". Ignore the footpath to your left and soon bear right at the fingerpost directing you in front of the farm towards "Cadgwith and Ruan Minor".

3. Cross a wall stile on the left beside a wooden gate and proceed along the top of a wide bank between arable fields with fine rural views ahead. Come off this raised footpath and climb a wall stile and keep to the left-hand side of the next field to another stile beside a metal gate. Briefly follow a track before bearing right onto a quiet lane. Stay on this lane, ignoring the footpath waymarked down a lane towards "Studio Colva", carrying on to some houses and a footpath fingerpost waymarking the route to "Cadgwith". The lane soon becomes an unmetalled trackway between houses and gradually descends down into Cadgwith Cove. Shortly, rejoin the outward route bearing left into the hamlet, downhill back to the inn.

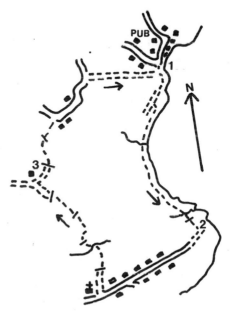

15

The Spaniards Inn, Cargreen

The peaceful raised terrace is the place to sit on summer days at this rambling old pub, charmingly situated on the banks of the River Tamar, with views across the river to the rolling fields of Devon. The original 400 year old cottages have been much extended at the side and back since becoming a pub some 80 years ago. The quaint façade and the intimate front bars are all that remains of the cottages, with the oak-framed lead paned windows – one of which was a church window – beams and huge stone fireplace. A real assortment of furniture fills the bars, from rustic style to church pews in the simple public bar and from modern oak tables and standard pub chairs to comfortable wall bench seating and pews in the long lounge bar and restaurant. There are superb estuary views from the windows of the latter bar. There are mooring facilities for those who wish to arrive by boat.

The pub is a free house efficiently run by Terry Haines. Four regularly changing real ales are available on hand pump and may include Bass, Dartmoor Best Bitter, Morland Old Speckled Hen and Wadworth 6X. Addlestones Cider is served on draught.

The snack menu of fresh sandwiches, half a French stick filled with chicken and garlic or ham and salad for example, are served all day in summer months. Afternoon cream teas are also available during this period. Between 12 noon and 2.30 p.m. and from 6.30 p.m. till 10 p.m. all year, a blackboard menu advertises the daily dishes. A wide ranging selection includes chilli, steak and mushroom pie, liver and bacon, beef stew, lamb tandoori, chicken baked in a cream mushroom and garlic sauce, various grills and a choice of fish – scampi, grilled sardines and baked lemon sole with a seafood sauce. Vegetarian meals are available such as vegetable curry and cheese and vegetable pizza. Sunday roasts are very popular and children have their own menu.

Weekday opening times in the winter are from 11 a.m. till 3 p.m. and from 6 p.m. till 11 p.m., 11 a.m. till 11 p.m. from April to September.

Children are very welcome inside, but dogs are only allowed in the public bar.
The inn has five letting bedrooms.
Telephone: (0752) 84283.

The village and inn are signposted from the A388, 3 miles north of Saltash.

Approx. distance of walk: 3½ miles. O.S. Map No. 201 SX 436/626.

The inn has a car park on the water's edge.

An enjoyable short walk along field paths and established tracks, with excellent Tamar views. The church at Landulph is worth a visit. Some of the tracks can be very muddy underfoot in the winter.

1. From the pub turn right up the village street – Fore Street, away from the river. At the telephone box turn left, then at the next junction, keep left downhill to the children's play area, on the bank of the river. Shortly, pass Penyoke Mill and take the waymarked footpath on your right and cross a stile. Follow the walled path gently uphill to another stile and yellow arrow. Proceed uphill on a defined path, with views back over the village and river opening up. Climb a stile by a gate, turn right along the hedge and soon pass to the side of a wooden gate, onto a hedged path. Head gradually downhill, away to your left there are excellent views down the Tamar to Brunel's bridge at Saltash. On reaching a lane, bear left downhill to Landulph Church.

2. Turn right by Landulph Church and follow a private road towards Marsh Farm. In a little way, turn left along a signed path and pass between the farm and a marshy area, along a defined path. Gradually climb uphill on an old path/bridleway (muddy) and bear left where it emerges with a wider trackway. Follow this to a lane. Turn right along this quiet metalled lane, with views down into a creek and Moditonham Quay, passing a driveway to a few houses before reaching a T-junction. Cross the lane and follow the arrowed path along a concreted drive. Pass between two properties to a wooden gate. Pass through the gate and keep to the left hand hedge to a stile in the corner. Keep left to a metal gate and pass through the farmyard of Grove farm to a lane.

3. Turn left, passing a house called St. Anns on your right, then shortly pass another driveway before taking the waymarked path on the right, through a small wooden gate. A defined path keeps to the right hand side of the field to a stile near a new house. Proceed down the right hand hedge of a field, with open views ahead over the river into Devon, to another stile. Cross the stile and bear half-right downhill across a large field to a metal gate and footpath marker post. Head towards a boat mooring area and the field corner to a stile. Climb the stile, drop down onto a lane beside a creek and turn right. Pass Cargreen Yacht Club and follow the lane back into the village. At the T-junction, turn left down Fore Street, back to the river bank and the pub.

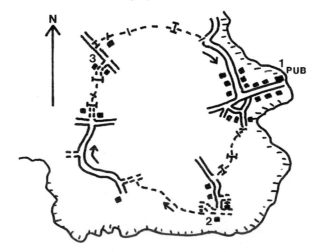

Trengilly Wartha Inn, Constantine

Built in 1800 as a farmhouse the Trengilly Wartha only became a pub in 1950. Today it is a smart country "auberge" style inn set in a remote wooded valley above Polpenwith Creek on the Helford River. Literally translated the name means "the settlement above the trees" and from the terrace and peaceful garden there are views across some of the inn's six acres of meadowland and down the valley over the trees towards the river. The large main bar has exposed stone walls and beams, high backed settles, polished heavy wooden tables and a few smaller tables and stools. A large woodburner warms the bar in winter. Up a couple of steps is the comfortable main eating area with some winged settles and tables. A front games room with pool table is ideal for children.

This welcoming free house is very well run by the owners Nigel Logan and Michael Maguire and their wives. Real ale is taken seriously here, at least five beers from breweries countrywide are served on hand pump and may include Batemans XXXB, Dartmoor Best Bitter, Tetleys, Courage Directors and Burton Ale.

Bar food is consistently good, the varied menu and daily changing specials are chalked up on blackboards above the bar. Starters range from Greek salad and home-made courgette and almond soup served with granary bread to smoked haddock pâté and seafood strudel. Main dishes include a large choice of salads especially local seafood, pasta dishes, chilli, filled jacket potatoes, Trengilly cassoulet, lemon sole and for vegetarians: raised vegetable pie, ratatouille and vegetable pasty. Desserts include pear and almond tart. A separate menu is available for children. Barbeques are held in summer under the vine covered pergola on the terrace. There is also an excellent restaurant serving a value-for-money set menu. Bar food is served between 12 noon and 2.15 p.m. and from 6.30 p.m. till 9.30 p.m.

Children are allowed in the family room, games room and in the lounge and there is no objection to dogs in the bars.

Weekday opening times are from 11 a.m. till 2.30 p.m. and 6 p.m. till 11 p.m.

Overnight accommodation is available.

Telephone: (0326) 40332.

Inn is situated in the hamlet of Nancenoy, 1 mile south of Constantine which is signed from the B3291 Penryn to Gweek road.

Approx. distance of walk: 4 miles. O.S. Map No. 204 SW 731/282.

The inn has a large car park.

An enjoyable walk through woodland and along farm tracks and paths with superb views across the Helford River valley on the return route.

1. From the car park at the inn return along the driveway, turn left onto the lane and proceed downhill crossing a small brook at the bottom before ascending the steep hill ahead. Remain on the tiny lane down to a small river bridge then shortly turn left at Polwheveral Cottage onto a gravel driveway passing a garage into woodland. Follow the narrow pathway up the tranquil river valley, bear left onto an unmetalled trackway to a lane.

2. Turn left, cross a bridge near Constantine Youth Club and immediately turn right then left to follow the driveway to "Long Barn". The track passes Long Barn on the right and continues up valley, a very enjoyable stretch of trackway. Where the track turns sharp right bear off left into the woodland onto a well established footpath across the brook then along the beautiful wooded valley side. Shortly, at a crossroads of paths go straight across passing a stone with "1988" inscribed on it and proceed uphill passing some stone steps on the right. Bear left onto a trackway and follow this through a quarry yard to a lane.

3. Turn left, then soon turn right (not signed) onto a track. Pass through a metal gate then immediately left through another gate and follow the track uphill beside the hedge. Join a more defined track, keep to the right of a large house and proceed uphill bearing right past the farmyard and shortly bear left, soon to pass a wooden house on the right. On reaching a narrow lane turn left downhill, proceed across the crossroads towards "Constantine" and remain on the lane into the village.

4. Turn right beside a thatched cottage towards the small village car park and bear left along the lane in front of the church with fine rural views away to the right. Keep right at the next junction and remain on the lane between houses which soon becomes a narrow pathway beside the doctors surgery. Cross a stone stile and head straight across the next three fields and wall stiles on a well defined path with panoramic views over the Helford valley and open countryside. Drop down onto a quiet lane, turn right and follow the lane back to the inn.

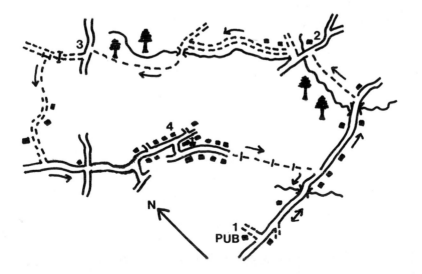

Old Albion, Crantock

This attractive 400 year old inn is situated at the end of a quiet lane next to the lych gate of Crantock church. It is probably named after a schooner built a mile or so away in Gannel shipyard when Crantock was a prosperous seaport some 500 years ago. The present pub sign shows H.M.S. Albion, a 90-gun ship launched at Plymouth in 1842. The quaint picture-postcard exterior of whitewashed stone and low thatch, resplendent with colourful flower beds and hanging baskets hides quite surprisingly an open plan layout. Character and charm has not been lost in the main bar which has boarded and beamed ceilings, cushioned wall bench seating and the odd old settle with leather upholstery. Red cushioned stools surround small wooden tables and various horse brasses, naval badges, plates and local prints and photographs of bygone years adorn the walls. Two open fires warm the bar, one is a large inglenook decorated with odd bits of brassware and visible in the right hand corner is the old smugglers hole which supposedly led to Crantock beach. Each fireplace has its own pasty oven. A lower bar has a variety of scrubbed tables and chairs, a shelf displaying old pots, bottles and china plates and is a popular eating area. There are a couple of benches in front of the pub on the lane and a small garden with barbeque is located just off the parking area.

The inn is a Courage pub run by licensee Andrew Bown with Courage Best Bitter being the only real ale served on draught.

Bar food is served seven days a week from 12 noon till 2 p.m. and from 7 p.m. till 9.30 p.m., although these times are flexible during the height of the season. The menu includes the usual snacks such as lasagne, scampi, pasties, $\frac{1}{4}$ roast chicken with french fries, a range of filled jacket potatoes, sandwiches and ploughmans. Blackboard specials include ham, egg and chips, steaks, gammon and salads. Apple pie and chocolate fudge cake are usually available for dessert. Children have their own menu.

Families are welcome in the pub, dogs too.

Weekday opening times are from 11 a.m. till 11 p.m all year round.

Accommodation is available in the adjacent self-catering cottage.

Telephone: (0637) 830243.

Village signed off the A3075 just south of Newquay.

Approx. distance of walk: 5 miles. O.S. Map No. 200 SW 790/606.

Parking is limited at the pub. There are a few spaces in the village, otherwise it maybe necessary to use the large beach car park and walk back up the lane to the pub.

A most enjoyable walk, across a diverse landscape of duneland, rocky headlands, common land and beside sandy surfing beaches including Holywell Bay, the largest bay on this stretch of coast. Easy going except for the sandy path across the dunes into Holywell and ideal for all the family.

1. Turn right on leaving the pub to follow the lane to the left by the church lych gate onto a rough track. At the end turn left up the lane and shortly turn right along a pitted track and waymarked path. Pass a few houses then proceed ahead onto a footpath towards Crantock Beach. Once at the dunes turn left along the coast path which soon bears right along the edge of a field with views over the dunes and the vast sandy beach towards Pentire Head East. Cross a stile remaining on the coast path, soon to cross the base of the hotel's lawn. Head out around Pentire Point West where the path becomes gentle, wide and grassy.

2. Shortly descend into Porth Joke ("Joke is a corruption of the Cornish word 'gwic', meaning creek") a remote picturesque beach in a sheltered cove and climb two stiles before crossing the wooden footbridge over the incoming stream. Cross the head of the beach then begin the gradual climb up around Kelsey Head. The headland is covered in purple thrift in summer. The grassy path passes the low bank and shallow ditch of an Iron Age cliff castle before the vast expanse of Holywell Bay comes into view with its fine dunes rising up to 200 feet

behind the beach. Follow the path down to a wooden gate onto a boardwalk and keep to the sandy path across the dunes inland to the car park and shop/cafe in Holywell.

3. Turn left in front of some houses and follow the sandy path across the edge of the dunes and shortly beside a golf course. Go through a wooden gate then keep to the right hand edge of a vast grazing area known as the "Kelseys". Pass through another gate on the right at the end of the golf course and turn left along the wire fence. Shortly, bear off right and cross the trackway from the house to the right onto Cubert Common. Soon drop down beside a wire fence towards the house and campsite visible in the valley. Bear right along a track pass the house on the left, go through a metal gate onto a lane and bear left uphill following the waymarked route to "Crantock". Pass the farmhouse and camp site remaining on the lane shortly to turn right onto the lane into Crantock. Cross the lane, soon to cross a stile on the left onto a grassy path downhill towards Crantock beach. At the beach rejoin the outward route inland back to the pub.

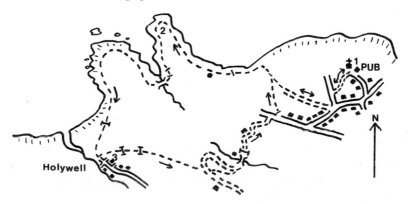

Holywell

The Crows Nest, Crows Nest

This delightful old inn lies tucked away in a peaceful little hamlet on the southern slopes of Bodmin Moor, an area rich in fascinating relics. Behind the pub the open moorland is scattered with old mine workings and engine houses and close by are a number of more ancient relics such as the megalithic tomb called Trethevy Quoit, Bronze Age stone circles and various prehistoric tumuli. The inn however is a little more recent, beginning life as a mine captain's house when the mine was in its heyday. It was also the pay office and the bell which summoned the miners is still in place above one of the windows. The miners were paid in part with Crows Nest money, so ale was sold from the office, it being the only place they could spend it. Today, the pub consists of long, narrow low beamed bar which is divided in the centre and a warm welcome is guaranteed. The left hand side has lots of horse stirrups, bits and spurs hanging from its heavy dark beams, old local photographs, an assortment of tables, wall benches and captains chairs plus an unusual table created from a large pair of bellows. A large log fire warms this bar. The dining area is comfortable and has a table and bench seating in a massive disused inglenook. Picnic tables line the outdoor terrace.

The pub is owned by the St. Austell brewery and serves their Tinners ale and the stronger Hicks Special.

Bar food is available seven days a week from 12 noon till 2.30 p.m. and 7 p.m. till 10 p.m. There is always a daily special which may be an excellent home-made steak and kidney pie, served with vegetables. The main menu ranges from a hearty soup, such as ham and vegetable, Cornish shell bake, fish pie, ham and chips, spicy pork with rice, beef curry, lasagne and a good ploughmans. Puddings are traditional and include home-made spotted dick and treacle sponge.

Children under 14 are not allowed in the bar and dogs must be left outside.

Weekday opening times are from 11.30 a.m. till 3.30 p.m. and 6 p.m. till 11 p.m.

Telephone: (0579) 45930.

Village and pub are signposted from the B3254 north of Liskeard.

Approx. distance of walk: 3½ miles. O.S Map No. 201 SX 264/693.

The inn has a large car park

A short interesting walk exploring field paths, quiet lanes, the village of St. Cleer and Trethevy Quoit on the southern edge of Bodmin Moor.

1. Turn left out of the pub onto the lane and soon turn right down the first metalled lane. Follow the lane past a place called Tinners Gate and cross a small brook. Remain on this quiet lane to a junction. Bear right, back across the brook and begin to climb uphill. Near the top where the lane veers right, bear off left towards Trethevy farm. By the stone cottage bear right up three slate steps and pass a milking shed to a metal gate and pasture. Bear half-left across the field with superb views over rolling Cornish countryside. Head towards the far left hand corner and pass through a small metal gate. Proceed diagonally left downhill to another visible gate in the right hand corner and bear half-right towards a tree in the hedge, looking out for a metal kissing gate. Bear left down the centre of the next field with the village of Tremar ahead. Go through a metal gate and join a concrete, then metalled lane beside a farm and follow it down into the hamlet.

2. At a T-junction turn left, gently climb uphill before turning right along Tremar Lane, signed to St. Cleer. This shortly narrows to become a delightful lane. Follow this into the moorstone village of St. Cleer and its stout-walled 15th century church which has an intriguing Victorian stained glass window depicting eleven female saints. Turn right at the T-junction opposite the church and follow the lane downhill to the striking rather Gothic-looking chapel built over St. Cleer's Holy Well, restored in 1864. Proceed along the lane out of the village to a T-junction.

3. Cross the road onto a stony track towards a house called Holmfield. Just before the metal gates bear left through a small wooden gate onto a stony walled path and gently climb uphill. Go through another gate to join a fine grassy green lane which leads you to a few houses and a lane. The impressive Neolithic chamber tomb of Trethevy Quoit with its massive 10 ton capstone lies in the field to your left. Turn left along the lane, the old copper mine workings visible on the moor to the right. At a telograph pole cross a stone stile and pass through a gap in the wall into pasture and follow a defined path to the far left hand corner. Climb a stone stile beside a gate and drop down onto a lane. Turn right back into Crows Nest and the pub.

The Earl of St. Vincent, Egloshayle

Hidden away in the old part of this rambling village, which merges with Wadebridge, is the Earl of St. Vincent, a characterful 15th century white painted inn which was originally built as a boarding house for the masons who built the church and named after one of Nelson's Admirals. Open the door and its like walking into Aladdin's Cave, for the main bar is crammed full with interesting memorabilia. A warm and relaxing atmosphere has been created by the landlords passion for collecting antiques and furnishing his pub with them. Beneath the low, heavily beamed ceiling every wall is adorned with various prints, paintings and sketches. Every other surface displays clocks of all kinds, from grandfather clocks to antique ball-bearing clocks – all of which are in good working order. Pieces of china decorate all the tables, shelves and window ledges. A delightful mix of tables and chairs furnish the bar including honey coloured church pews, pine settles, large oval table and up to six cosy armchairs with cushions, some of which face the open fire. An intimate little snug room resounds with ticking clocks and has some antique carved chairs. The small terraced garden with picnic benches is ablaze with colourful flowers in the summer.

The inn is owned by the St. Austell brewery and lovingly cared for by Anne and Edward Connolly. Well kept Tinners Ale and Hicks Special are served on hand pump.

Bar food is served seven days a week from 12 noon till 2 p.m. and 7.30 p.m. till 9.30 p.m. A blackboard displays the daily specials which may include smoked salmon, scallops, fillet steak, half roast duck, breast of chicken filled with lobster and prawns, lemon sole, liver and bacon casserole, pork chops and a couple of vegetarian dishes. The main menu features a selection of grills, which are very popular, a range of fish dishes and a choice of salads – ham, beef, prawn or cheese. Home-made puddings include treacle tart.

Well behaved children are welcome in the bar if they eating.

Weekday opening times are from 11 a.m. till 3 p.m. and 6.30 p.m. till 11 p.m.

Telephone: (0208) 814807.

Village centre is signposted off the A389, just south east of Wadebridge.

Approx. distance of walk: 6 miles. O.S. Map No. 200 SX 001/720.

The inn has a car park, but if the barrier is closed there is some limited space near the church.

A fairly long yet enjoyable walk along established tracks and through woodland, returning to Wadebridge along the peaceful Camel Trail—once the route of the Bodmin to Padstow railway, which ran parallel with the River Camel. It is mostly easy going underfoot.

1. From the pub turn right to the T-junction and turn left, following the lane past the church to the main road. Cross over, turn right and walk along the pavement towards Wadebridge, with the River Camel away to your left. In a short way turn left and enter a small recreation/park area. Follow the raised tarmac riverside path round to the footbridge over the Camel. Cross the bridge and turn left. On reaching a footpath fingerpost bear off right onto a track, waymarked Treraven. The Camel Trail is signed straight on. Pass to the rear of some houses and follow this established hedged track uphill, climbing out of the valley. Approaching Treraven farm, bear left with the track in front of the house, then keep right to follow the established tree-lined track. Pass through a gate and proceed ahead along this old green lane, which gradually ascends through farmland, eventually reaching a lane.

2. Proceed ahead along the lane for a short distance and turn left at the crossroads into the village of Burlawn. At the T-junction in the village centre turn left, pass the village pump, then follow the lane right and begin to descend into a valley. Continue past Hus-

tyn Mill, cross the stream and shortly turn left along a stony track and enter a coniferous plantation area. With tall pine trees to your right and a river valley away to the left remain on this track, which soon curves right. The River Camel now is visible to your left. Follow this well defined woodland path, soon to merge with a forest track and proceed ahead until reaching a narrow lane.

3. Turn left and cross Polbrock Bridge over the River Camel. Just before the old railway bridge cross a stile on your left and drop down some wooden steps onto the disused railway—The Camel Trail. Turn left and follow this level, well surfaced track, parallel to the river. The trail passes through peaceful woodland stretches, providing good chances to view the abundant wildlife. The railway was built in 1834 to carry sea sand from the estuary to Bodmin, returning with granite and china clay which was shipped out of Wadebridge. In 1899 the line from Wadebridge to Padstow was laid, starting the route of the Atlantic Coast express which carried holidaymakers to the west country until its closure in the 1960's. Remain on the trail along the river valley back to the footbridge over the Camel and retrace your steps back to the inn.

Fishermans Arms, Golant

The charm of the Fishermans Arms is in its setting, nestling among fishermans cottages in the tiny riverside village of Golant. Situated close to the river's edge this cream painted cottage is a real picture in summer with hanging baskets and flower boxes adorning its exterior. The terrace and well kept garden enjoy fine peaceful views across the River Fowey, certainly the place to relax with a drink on a summers evening. The pub is very popular with the sailing fraternity, many sailing up from Fowey, especially when high tide corresponds with opening time. There are two bars, a tiny simply furnished room which serves as the family room and a large bar which overlooks the garden and river. A small flagged stone area fronts the bar with a comfortable carpeted dining area to one side and a tiled floor section furnished with a mix of tables and chairs to the other. It has a very homely feel with a fish tank in one wall, a piano and an excellent collection of local prints and photographs including pictures of naval ships, bygone fishing days and local characters. An open log fire warms this bar in winter.

The pub is owned by Ushers and presently serves on hand pump Courage Best Bitter, Ushers Best Bitter and the strong Founders Ale.

Bar food is served seven days a week with a barbeque every Sunday evening in the summer. Good hearty snacks are served from noon at lunchtimes and from 7 p.m. in the evenings. Choose from the standard menu or from the specials chalked up weekly on the blackboard. Dishes include cottage pie, fishermans pie, steak and chips, seafood lasagne, chicken kiev, steak and kidney pie, ham, egg, and chips, huge pasties, plaice and scampi platters and a range of freshly cut sandwiches, ploughmans, salads and well filled jacket potatoes.

Children are welcome in the small separate bar and there is no objection to dogs in the bars.

Weekday opening times are from 11 a.m. till 3 p.m. and from 6 p.m. till 11 p.m.
Telephone: (072683) 2453.

The delightful village of Golant is signposted off the B3269, four miles south of Lostwithiel.

Approx. distance of walk: 3 miles. O.S. Map No. 200 SX 123/545.

Parking is limited at the pub, it is best to park 100 yards along the lane in the parking area near the public toilets. You are warned not to park beside the estuary at the pub as the lane is cut off at particularly high tides.

A short but very enjoyable and scenic walk with good views across the Fowey and over rolling Cornish countryside. Parts of the route follow the "Saints Way", a cross country walk between Padstow and Fowey once travelled by Welsh and Irish saints of the Dark Ages between AD400 and 700. Suitable for the whole family, mostly easy going although one track may be very muddy in wet weather.

1. From the Fishermans Arms turn right uphill, passing quaint cottages before turning first left along a lane. Keep left taking the lower tarmac drive at the "private road" sign. At the end join a narrow path around the back of the Cormorant Hotel, which is waymarked with the yellow arrow and black cross of "The Saints Way". Keep to this bracken-edged path with views up and down the splendid Fowey river and across into Penpoll Creek opposite. The path soon descends, bearing right into a peaceful wooded creek, cross the brook and turn right to follow the signed path to "Fowey" uphill.

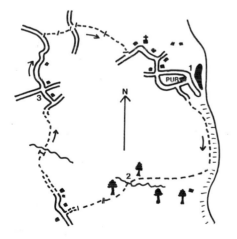

2. The path passes through beautiful beech woodland along the edge of the brook then proceeds up the valley side to cross two stiles. Follow the arrows uphill across a field to another stile to join a trackway beside farm buildings. Do not follow the "Saints Way" signs left, but bear right along a metalled lane towards "Lanherriot Farm". Before reaching the farmhouse bear left onto a wide muddy trackway and shortly head downhill along an ancient high-banked pathway into a wooded valley. Pass through a gate, cross a brook and proceed uphill soon to bear left onto a trackway. Follow this round to a metalled lane.

3. Turn left and on reaching a crossroads go straight across onto a narrow lane. Remain on this hedged lane downhill untill reaching the waymarked route on the right across a stile. Now back on the "Saints Way", bear half-right uphill across the field to a stile in the hedge where fine views back across rolling farmland can be enjoyed. Keep to the left hand edge of the next field, cross two stiles and a lane and proceed along a trackway through a field soon to bear right to a stile in the hedge. Cross the corner of the field, then follow the left-hand edge to a stile and turn left onto a lane. Pass St. Sampson parish church on the left and head down a steep hill back into Golant. At the bottom of the hill go across the crossroads, past the Post Office and follow the lane downhill back to the pub.

The sketch maps in this book are not necessarily to scale but have been drawn to show the maximum amount of detail.

The Barley Sheaf, Gorran Churchtown

The Barley Sheaf was built in 1837 as a pub by a local landowner. The story is that he had been barred from all the neighbouring pubs for drunkenness, so in order to enjoy his drink he decided to build his own. There is a wide staircase within the pub and at one time this is where the local tenants had to queue to pay their rents to the landowners who were in the large room upstairs. The pub is reputed to be haunted. The rather austere stone facade is mellowed by colourful window boxes in spring and summer while inside the atmosphere is one of a friendly village local. The open plan high-ceilinged bars are simply furnished with cushioned bench seating, chairs and stools around scrubbed wooden tables. Old photographs of Gorran Haven adorn the walls in both the main bar area and in the food ordering and eating area. To the rear of the pub up a few steps is a sheltered garden complete with childrens play area and barbeque.

The pub is a free house enthusiastically run by the owners Andy and Gill Thomson. A good range of well conditioned real ales are available on hand pump and may include St. Austell Tinners Ale, Cornish Original, Bass, Castle Eden Ale and Wadworth 6X. A local cider is also available in summer.

A comprehensive range of bar food is served seven days a week from 12 noon till 2 p.m. and in the evening from 7 p.m. till 10 p.m. with a traditional roast on Sundays. Snacks include sandwiches, toasties, ploughmans and filled jacket potatoes. Heartier meals on offer are steaks, fishermans pie, cottage pie, chicken kiev, lemon sole and a range of salads from the salad bar to accompany local crab, prawns, mackerel and a choice of meats. Vegetarian meals include quiche, pasty, cauliflower and broccoli gratin and a vegetable lasagne. A few daily specials are chalked up on a blackboard.

Children and dogs are most welcome inside the pub.

Weekday opening times are from 12 noon till 3 p.m. and from 6 p.m. till 11 p.m. Telephone: (0726) 843330.

Village lies 1 mile north west of Gorran Haven.

Approx. distance of walk: 5½ miles. O.S. Map No. 204 SW 999/423.

The pub has a large car park opposite.

A delightful walk across meadowland towards Mevagissey followed by a scenic and coastal stretch to Gorran Haven with magnificent views across Mevagissey Bay towards Fowey. Although undulating the going is easy underfoot and fairly dry.

1. Turn right on leaving the pub, pass the general stores and turn left along a T-road beside the church which shortly bears left around the churchyard following the way-marked route to "Galowgras Mill 1 mile". The lane soon gives way to pot-holed track then just before the gateway to Cotna House turn right across a stone stile onto a well defined path across the field ahead. Go over the stile in the hedge, bear slightly left across another field to a stile with fine rural views. Proceed half right gradually downhill to a stone stile to the right of a gate and descend sharply into a valley ahead. On nearing the bottom cross a stile on the right, keep to the path passing an oak tree downhill through a wooden gate. Cross a small brook and follow the path across lush meadowland along the valley side to a stile and enter woodland. The path keeps to the right of a small lake and reedbeds before crossing a stile beside a gate. Turn sharp left onto a track, cross the brook and bear right at the house ahead onto a signed footpath beside the wall.

2. Go through a metal gate, cross a tiny brook and remain on the defined path across the valley side, through a gap in the wall then gradually up the valley side towards the buildings ahead. Pass through a gate onto a trackway keeping to the left of the farmhouse, across the yard to follow the arrowed route up the farm drive to a lane. Turn left then turn right at the corner onto a signed pathway downhill, keeping left along a pitted track to a road. Turn right and proceed downhill into Portmellon Cove.

3. Begin to ascend out of the cove then shortly bear left into Chapel Point Lane and join the waymarked coast path. Beyond the houses on the left there are wide open views across Mevagissey Bay to Black Head. Follow the coast path symbol off to the left onto a grassy path, cross a stile and head towards the buildings at Chapel Point. Cross the driveway, bear left across a stile near a small boathouse and shortly pass through a wooden swing gate to follow the narrow path around the headland edge. The path

undulates up and down the cliffs with views ahead to Gorran Haven then follows the left hand edge of fields close to the cliff edge across stiles before joining a metalled lane beside Perhaver Cottage on the edge of Gorran Haven.

4. Turn right then right at the end into Cliff Road and follow the signed path "Trewollack". Bear right into the first cul-de-sac keeping right onto the waymarked path around the back of houses to a double stile. Proceed uphill bearing left at the hedge to a gate and join a trackway which shortly passes through Trewollack Farm to a lane. Turn left through the hamlet of Trewollack keeping right signposted "Gorran". At a junction of lanes at Bell Hill turn right onto a narrow lane "unsuitable for motors", then at a T-junction go across the road through a gate onto an old trackway. In a short distance cross a stone stile in the hedge on the left and head towards the church keeping to the right hand edge downhill to another stile. Follow the narrow path uphill to a lane and bear left onto the outward route back to the pub.

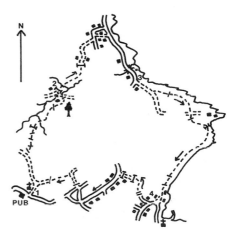

29

The Rising Sun, Gunnislake

This attractive little whitewashed cottage was built in the 17th century and enjoys a superb position overlooking the picturesque wooded Tamar valley. The well tended terraced front is a summer favourite among customers for the unrivalled valley views. Inside, a warm welcome is assured in the three homely drinking areas. The main bar area has a part-boarded ceiling, exposed stone walls, darkwood pub furniture and a roaring log fire in the winter. A few pictures, jugs and plates hang there, but the real collection of china, photographs and pictures adorn the other areas. All sorts of jugs, chamber pots, ornamental plates, cups and saucers line the ceiling or decorate the walls. Comfortable, red velvet padded seats are arranged around darkwood tables and are popular with diners.

The pub is a free house dispensing an excellent range of real ales on hand pump, such as Courage Best Bitter, Fullers London Pride, Bass, St. Austell Hicks Special and Eldridge Pope Blackdown Porter. Inch's Cider is also served on draught.

A short blackboard menu displays the range of freshly prepared dishes that are available each day. Start with creamy prawn pots or a goulash soup, followed by appetising main courses which may include pork fillet Diane, beef and ale pie, whole grilled bass or rump steak with a pepper sauce. All are served with fresh vegetables and potatoes. The vegetarian option may be mushroom stroganoff. Desserts range from apple pie to various ice creams and sorbets. For those in search of a snack, sandwiches are always available. Bar food is served daily from 12 noon till 2.30 p.m. and 6.30 p.m. till 10 p.m.

Children are welcome in the back room and dogs are allowed in on a lead.

Weekday opening times are from 11 a.m. till 2.30 p.m. and 5 p.m. till 11 p.m.

Telephone: (0822) 832201.

Gunnislake is situated 5 miles west of Tavistock on the A390. The pub is located along Calstock Road, on the edge of the village.

Approx. distance of walk: 3½ miles. O.S. Map No. 201 SX 433/712.

The pub has a car park at the rear as well as a few spaces in the front.

This short ramble explores the wooded Tamar valley, following the peaceful riverside path and returns along quiet country lanes. There is a long climb out of the valley. Good footwear is essential as the paths and tracks can be extremely muddy after wet weather.

1. Turn right on leaving the pub and follow the lane downhill into the valley. On reaching a house on the right called Morwell View, bear off left onto a track and head steeply downhill to the river. Pass the house on your left, following the track round to the river's edge. Turn left onto the riverside path, pass in front of the house and keep to this established path (can be muddy if the river has recently flooded). The path at first runs parallel to an old canalised section of the river, which at one time was the main route for transporting materials in and out of the area. Shortly, merge with a track, pass in front of some cottages on your left, then bear right in front of two more cottages to rejoin the riverside path (yellow arrow). Pass a weir and follow this delightful path along the bank to a junction with the road at Newbridge.

2. The bridge over the Tamar was built in the 16th century and was the lowest road bridge crossing until the bridge at Saltash was built in 1961. Cross the road, pass in front of a garage, following the waymarked footpath up a tarmac track. At a junction of three paths at Hawkmoor Cottage, keep ahead with the yellow arrow along the track. Shortly, at a fork of three tracks take the middle track (yellow arrow on post) and enter Clitters Wood. The track (can be muddy) gradually descends back towards the banks of the river. The path eventually climbs away from the river. At a fork in the path, it is worth bearing right onto a path that briefly crosses an area of old mine workings. It allows good views of the river and the remains of where tin, copper, arsenic and wolfram were mined. Return to the main path and climb sharply uphill to a lane.

3. Turn left along the narrow lane and climb steadily uphill into the tiny hamlet of Dimson. At a T-junction turn left, then on reaching a crossroads keep ahead into Chapel Lane. Follow the lane for a little way, before turning left into Hoopers Lane. Proceed downhill on this very narrow lane, bearing right around the perimeter of a small school to a T-junction. Turn right, then almost immediately left opposite the café and walk down to the traffic lights opposite the Tavistock Hotel in Gunnislake. Cross over the main road, turn right and follow the pavement to where Calstock Road branches off to the left, opposite the Cornish Inn. Remain on this lane, through the village back to the Rising Sun.

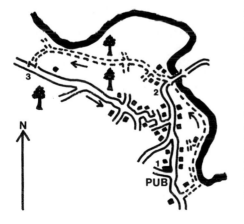

The Black Swan, Gweek

The Black Swan was built at the turn-of-the-century as a hotel to serve what was once a busy port importing coal and timber for the mines and was known as the Gweek Inn. Today, the old quays have become small boat yards for repairs and construction and the welcoming Black Swan remains popular with the thousands of visitors that come to see the seals at the famous Seal Sanctuary just along the road. Inside the whitewashed exterior lies a modern, carpeted open plan bar which is split into two main areas both furnished with dark wood tables and chairs and comfortable, plush wall benches which line the half-stone and half-pine panelled walls. A large wood burner warms one of the areas in the winter and what was once a fireplace in the small area by the bar is now filled with three beer barrels. The walls are decorated with various badges and photographs given to the pub by servicemen from nearby R.N.A.F. Culdrose, as well as photographs of Cornish wrecks and other boats. A few books adorn a number of small shelves around the pub. The head of the creek and the boat yard can be viewed from the windows and from the few tables and chairs to the side of the pub.

The Black Swan is a Whitbread pub well run for the past five years by Charles Edwards with a choice of three real ales on draught, Flowers I.P.A., Castle Eden Ale and West Country Pale Ale.

Good home-cooked food, served between 12 noon and 2.30 p.m. and 7 p.m. till 9 p.m., is available seven days a week. On the menu are a range of ploughmans served with local crab, ham, cheeses and a pâté, ham and prawn salads, sirloin steak, trout meuniere, various omelettes and a choice of vegetarian dishes such as stuffed peppers. The ever changing specials board may include chilli with rice, tuna and smoky bacon lasagne, crab salad and home-made pasties. Ham rolls are good, expect half a French stick! Fruit crumble and fudge cake may be the days desserts.

There is a separate room for children which also has a pool table. Dogs are welcome into the pub.

Weekday opening times are from 11 a.m. till 3 p.m. and 6 p.m. till 11 p.m.
Telephone: (0326) 22502.

Village is signed off the A394 at Trewannack 1½ miles north east of Helston.

Approx. distance of walk: 3 miles. O.S. Map No. 203 SW 706/268.

There is a large car park to the rear of the pub.

A scenic walk across meadows and along wide tracks, suitable for the whole family.

1. Leave the pub, turn left towards the creek, cross the bridge remaining on the road passing the boat yard on the left. Shortly, cross another bridge with fine wooded creek views and turn immediately right along a metalled lane which soon turns into an old cobbled lane passing a few isolated cottages. Cross a stone stile beside a metal gate onto a defined pathway along the right hand edge of the field. Pass through a metal gate then bear diagonally left downhill into a tranquil wooded valley, an ideal spot to view buzzards soaring over the valley sides. Go through a metal gate in the left hand corner near the valley bottom and keep forward along the base of the field near the brook.

2. Soon enter a thicket and bear left across what can be a muddy area to a green metal swing gate in the hedgerow. Proceed across the field ahead, pass through a metal gate and turn right onto an old green lane between two hedges which is full of wild flowers in early summer. The grassy pathway soon gives way to an old lane, remain on this downhill through a metal gate and shortly bear right in front of a barn passing a few isolated houses before joining a quiet country lane.

3. Turn right following the lane uphill and in ¼ mile where the lane bears round to the left take the unmetalled lane off to the right (not waymarked). In a short distance where the main track bears right towards a farmhouse proceed straight on along a peaceful unmetalled track affording beautiful rural views across the valley to Culdrose and Goonhilly Earth Station away to the right, eventually turn right onto a lane and head downhill into Gweek passing the sports field on the right. At the T-junction opposite the creek and boat yard turn left back across the river bridge to the pub.

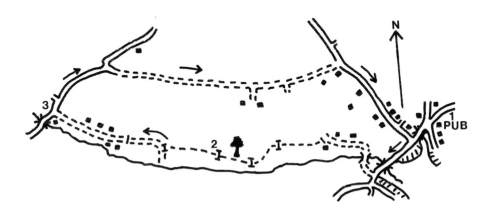

The Shipwrights Arms, Helford

The picturesque village of Helford straggles beside a tidal creek on the south bank of the peaceful wood-fringed waters of the Helford River. At the end of the village near the passenger ferry lies the Shipwights Arms idyllically set on the river bank with glorious terraced gardens dropping down to the waters edge. Built in 1795 as a farmhouse with later shipwright connections this attractive thatched pub is popular with both yachting types and visitors. The palm trees and colourful flower-filled terraced garden is the main attraction especially when the summer barbeque is well under way. If its raining the interior is equally as special; traditional and unspoilt with a black panelled bar, large woodburning stove, cushioned wall seats, oak settles in the small eating area away from the bar and is full of nautical bits and pieces, a ship's wheel, lamps, a display of knots and drawings of local fishermen line the walls.

The inn is a Whitbread pub efficiently run over the past five years by licensees Charles Herbert and Brandon Flynn and serving two real ales, Castle Eden Ale and Flowers I.P.A.

This is a very popular place to eat offering at lunchtime an excellent salad bar selection to choose from. Good portions of freshly prepared salads can accompany ham, stilton, cheddar, mackerel, smoked trout, beef, salmon or fresh local crab. Ploughmans lunches can also be made from the above meats. In the evenings a more comprehensive menu includes steak and kidney pie, beef in beer, char-grilled pork and steaks, half a roast chicken and more fishier fare such as local scallops, monkfish, crab and lobster. For pudding try the home-made treacle and nut tart or chocolate truffle torte. Excellent steaks and burgers for the children are prepared on the barbeque in the summer months. Food is served daily during the summer 12 noon till 2 p.m. and 7 p.m. till 9 p.m., in winter no food is available on Sunday and Monday evenings.

Children are welcome inside the pub if eating. Dogs must be kept on a lead.

Weekday opening times are from 11 a.m. till 2.30 p.m. and 6 p.m. till 11 p.m.

Telephone: (032623) 235.

Take the A3083 from Helston towards the Lizard turning left onto the B3293 for Coverack. Turn left for Newtown St. Martin and follow signs for Manaccan and Helford.

Approx. distance of walk: 2¾ miles. O.S. Map No. 204 SW 758/262.

Parking is difficult at the pub, in summer the village is restricted to pedestrians only. It is advisable to park in the car park on the edge of the village.

A short, very peaceful walk incorporating the evocative Frenchmans Creek, a smugglers hideaway made famous by Daphne du Maurier's novel and best seen at high tide when the merging of water and vegetation is so blurred by the fallen trees that one can imagine being in the Everglades.

1. Leave the pub, keep left of the tiny car park and turn left onto a track opposite the route to the Helford Ferry. Proceed uphill passing cottages on the left then turn right at the yellow route marker through a gate, pass a garage on the right to a metal gate and cross a driveway. Follow the marker arrow downhill through woodland into Penarvon Cove (NT), cross the top of the beach and bear right at the white stone cottage for a short circular woodland route around Pengwedhen with fine views of the Helford River and passing the tiny St. Francis' Chapel before returning to Penarvon Cove.

2. Bear right in front of the white cottage onto a trackway uphill, pass through a gate then at the top of the hill turn right onto a track signed "Frenchmans Creek". Follow the track around to the left then downhill with open views up the Helford River shortly to turn left at a gate and private sign. Go down a few steps, cross a stile onto a well defined footpath through scrubland and soon descend into mature woodland beside Frenchmans Creek.

3. This is a very tranquil stretch of footpath along the creek edge with the opportunity to see Heron, Cormorants, Curlews and Shelduck especially when the tide has ebbed. Follow the creek inland for ½ mile before bearing left uphill onto a track and proceed uphill towards Kestle Farm soon to bear right around farm buildings to a lane. Cross the lane, enter the main yard passing the farmhouse on the left, go through a metal gate and follow the track ahead into a field. Keep left (waymarked) along the field edge crossing a stone stile in the corner and descend into woodland. Cross a small brook, turn left onto a wider path beneath a beech tree canopy heading gradually downhill through a peaceful valley. Shortly join a concrete driveway then turn left onto a lane back into Helford. Cross the creek remaining on the lane past the Post Office back to the pub.

The Halfway House Inn, Kingsand

The Halfway House is located in the twin villages of Kingsand and Cawsand, which owe their existance to fishing and smuggling. Until 1844 the villages and the pub were in different counties, as the tiny stream that runs under the pub was the ancient border between Celtic Cornwall and Saxon England, hence the name of the pub. The boundary is recorded on the house called Devon-Corn opposite the inn. The Halfway House is tucked among the narrow lanes and colour-washed houses of this quaint village and has recently been resurrected after a long period of closure, becoming a popular meeting place. The comfortably refurbished and carpeted bar has part exposed walls, a central stone fireplace with a warming woodburning stove, a mix of old pine and small copper topped tables surrounded by darkwood "pub" chairs and attractive fabrics. There is also a separate restaurant.

The inn is a free house serving three real ales – Flowers Original, Boddingtons and Castle Eden Ale.

The range of bar food is good with some interesting blackboard specials. A short snack menu offers quick and filling meals such as ham, egg and chips, chunky Cornish pasties, beefburgers, filled jacket potatoes and various ploughmans. The daily changing blackboard menu features fresh local fish in the summer months, including lobster. For starters there may be moules, home-made pâté or a freshly prepared soup followed by fish pie, bouillabaise, salmon steak in a tomato and basil sauce, chicken in white wine or a range of grills, especially steaks. Vegetarian options include vegetable chilli and spinach and lentil lasagne. Tarterau citron, chocolate mousse and shortbread tarts with raspberries and strawberries could well be on the dessert list. Bar food is served from 12 noon till 2 p.m. and from 7 p.m. till 9.45 p.m.

Children are welcome in the restaurant area and well behaved dogs are allowed in the bar.

Weekday opening times are from 12 noon (11 a.m. in summer) till 3 p.m. and 7 p.m. till 11 p.m. During July and August the pub may be open all day from 11 a.m. till 11 p.m.

The inn has five letting bedrooms.

Telephone: (0752) 822279

Kingsand lies off the B3247, signposted from the A374 Torpoint to A38 (Plymouth – Liskeard) road.

Approx. distance of walk: 6 miles. O.S. Map No. 201 SX 434/505.

There is a public car park (charge) beside the inn.

A fairly long, well signposted and easy going walk through the woodland and parkland of Mount Edgecumbe Country Park, following the coast path with views across Plymouth Sound to Plymouth.

1. From the pub walk straight up the main village street, turning right opposite the foodstore into Green Lane. Bear left past the Rising Sun, uphill into Lower Row and Devonport Hill. Proceed steeply up Devonport Hill, joining a waymarked path at its end, signed towards Maker Church. Keep right at a junction of paths, then shortly pass one of the old blockhouse forts that once guarded Plymouth Sound and curve left to join a lane. Turn right along the lane for a little way, then bear off left to a stile and signed path to Maker Church. Follow the path round the right hand edge of a field to a kissing gate and turn right along a lane. Bear left at the next junction, passing Maker farm and walk along a lane for about 100 yards. At a footpath sign on your left, cross a stile and follow a defined path along a line of telegraph poles to another stile. Head gently uphill to a stile to the left of a white house. Cross the driveway onto the path opposite. Go over a stile beside a gate, follow the left hand wall to another stile, then bear right along the field edge towards the church. Beyond the next stile keep ahead across grassland to the left of the church to a footpath fingerpost.
2. Cross the drive to Mount Edgecumbe car park and follow the path signed to Empacombe and Cremyll Ferry. Head downhill across grass to a small gate and cross the B-road into woodland. Descend and go straight across a wide track onto a zig-zag path. Cross a stile on your left at a fence, then head across pasture towards a creek. Drop down onto a track, bear left through a gate and cross the lane and stile to follow the signed path along the edge of a field, close to the estuary. Remain on this path with views across to Devonport Dockyard, pass the ruin of Tower Windmill and even-

tually reach the tiny harbour at Empacombe. Bear round left in front of a pink-washed house, and walk up the driveway to its left. Keep ahead onto a track where the drive bears right and proceed along the established path across stiles towards Cremyll. On reaching a track bear left and shortly arrive at the Cremyll Ferry.
3. Turn right and almost immediately bear off left at the coast path sign to follow the concrete drive through the gates to Mount Edgecumbe Country Park. Proceed up the main tree-lined drive and turn left at the end of the trees, passing beneath the mansion on your right and head towards the water's edge. At a crossroads of paths turn right and soon pass a mock temple by a pond and landscaped gardens. Climb uphill on a narrow path to a gate, then pass close to a folly ruin and follow coast path signs along the edge of Plymouth Sound, before climbing up into woodland. Pass through a wooden gate, bear left on merging with a track and pass under an old stone arch. Remain on this wide and level wooded track around Fort Picklecombe. At a fork, bear off left with coast path sign and head gently downhill, pass through a gate, then with open views towards Cawsand descend to a stile and a lane. Turn right, then left across a stile at the road corner and house onto a way-marked track, signed Cawsand. Follow this easy path with superb coastal views back into Kingsand, retracing steps past the Rising Sun on entering the village from the coast path.

The Ship, Lerryn

Lerryn is now a sleepy village divided by the tidal River Lerryn but years ago before road transport was mechanised the quays were rarely without heaps of roadstone, coal, grain, sand, limestone and timber, brought up from Fowey in 200 ton ships. The Ship was probably named during the villages heyday of river activity and a relic of these days, an old limekiln, can be seen opposite the village hall. The whitewashed stone Ship Inn, resplendent with hanging baskets and climbing roses, is situated just a stones throw away from the creekside. The oldest part is over 200 years old and in the past has been three old cottages and a butcher's shop with a slaughterhouse (now the cellar). Later it was a cider house selling farm cider. The public bar and games room have old slate floors, the extended and open plan lounge area is carpeted with modern tables and chairs, cushioned stools partly warmed by a large woodburner. There are horse brasses on the beams and numerous old village photographs decorate the walls. A homely and welcoming atmosphere pervades and the pub is busy with locals and holidaymakers. A sheltered back lawn has some picnic benches and a children's play area, while among the flower borders in front of the pub are two benches with village views.

The pub is a free house run by Howard and Mandy Packer. The well stocked bar always has a choice of three real ales available on hand pump which might include Courage Best Bitter, Bass and John Smiths Bitter.

A good range of bar food is available seven days a week. The varied menu is chalked up on a large blackboard and the home-made selection includes steak and ale pie, chicken and apricot pie, venison pie, beef escoril, sandwiches, various salads, steaks, pasties and ploughmans. Good vegetarian dishes include tagliatelle niçoise and wheat and walnut casserole. For pudding choose from apple and blackberry pie, gooseberry and honey pie or a variety of ice creams. Children have their own menu. Food is served from 12 noon till 2 p.m. and from 6 p.m. till 9 p.m. in the pub.

Both children and dogs are welcome in the pub.

Weekday opening times are from 11.30 a.m. till 3 p.m. and from 6 p.m. till 11 p.m. The inn has two letting bedrooms.

Telephone: (0208) 872374.

Village is signposted from the A390 in Lostwithiel.

Approx. distance of walk: 5 miles. O.S. Map No. 200 SX 140/570.

There is a public car park down beside the creek.

A peaceful and very enjoyable walk through woodland alongside the tranquil Lerryn creek and the River Fowey to the idyllic setting of St. Winnow Church on the river's edge. Parts of the church date from Norman times and there are good wagon roofs and some fine 16th century stained glass. The location has often been used for films, some of the scenes in the series "Poldark" were filmed here. There is also an interesting farming museum close to the church. The return route crosses farmland and affords open views of beautiful, rolling countryside.

1. Leave the pub and follow the lane through the village, across the narrow bridge at the head of the creek and turn left along a T-road. At the junction opposite a whitewashed stone cottage bear left down to the creek edge. At low tide it is possible to cross the creek from the car park via stepping stones. Follow the trackway beside the creek, keep right of the "Granary" and pass through a wooden gate into Ethy Woods (NT). The well established path follows the course of the creek through mature mixed woodland and is particularly beautiful at high tide. Shortly, the path bears right along a tributary creek and bear left at the post with yellow arrows waymarking the routes. Keep on the woodland path gradually climbing uphill and bear left onto a wide avenue through broom bushes. The footpath soon bears left off this track (yellow arrow) back down to the water's edge.

2. Soon rejoin the wide trackway which soon gives way to a narrower path through beautiful woodland as it rounds St. Winnow Point. Begin to descend, gradually emerging from the woodland, cross a stile then bear left along the edge of the field to another stile and head towards the church just visible amongst the trees ahead. Cross another stile and drop down onto the river bank. At low tide follow the path along the foreshore, up the slipway and into the churchyard. When the tide is high a diversion across the stile on the right into the orchard and out onto the lane beside the church may be necessary.

3. Leave the churchyard and shortly turn right along the signed path between a farmhouse and the small museum, passing through a gate onto a wide farm track bearing left steeply uphill through a second gate. At the top of this old green lane cross a stile

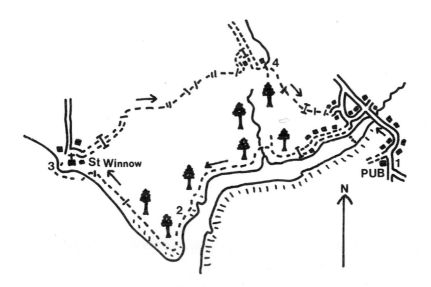

39

and follow the waymarked route diagonally across the field ahead with panoramic views across the River Fowey and open countryside opening out behind. Cross two stiles in the thick hedge, keep left along the bank to a stile beside a metal gate then bear right across the field to another stile and follow the yellow arrow markers to the left heading gradually downhill towards the woodland and a stile. Cross two stiles in the hedgerow, follow the left hand edge of the field downhill looking for a stile on the left before the woods. Cross this, proceed down the right hand side of the field and pass through a gateway on the right onto a trackway.

4. Turn right passing the ruins of St. Winnow Mill and cross its stream. The track climbs uphill, shortly bear left at a fork in the path and proceed up the steep hill through oak and beech woodland. Emerge from the wood, cross two stiles and keep ahead across grassland scattered with oak trees soon to pass through an old gateway. Keep the bank and fine mansion of Ethy on the left down to a stile. Proceed across the field to a stile to the right of the bungalows ahead. Turn left at the head of the cul-de-sac then turn right downhill along T-road into Lerryn. At the white cottage on the right either turn left to follow outward route back across the bridge to the pub or if the tide is low cross the stepping stones to the car park.

St. Winnow Church

Lerryn Creek

St. Michael's Mount

41

The White Hart, Ludgvan

The granite grey stone exterior of the White Hart belies the true age of this village local dating from the 14th century and reputed to be older than the adjacent church. Walk inside to a real old world unspoilt atmosphere in the main bar, two further small rooms and in a tiny intimate alcove. Ochre coloured walls, low beams and oil lamp lighting give the pub a dark, snug cottage-like atmosphere which is further enhanced by the mix of rustic tables and chairs that furnish the bars. Every shelf, nook and cranny is crammed full with bric-a-brac, jugs and mugs and tasteful prints adorn the walls. The small room to the left of the entrance has an old kitchen range, shelves with blue and white china plates and rustic furniture. Fine weather imbibing can be enjoyed in the peaceful garden to the rear or out front with views of the church. Unusual entertainment at the White Hart comes in the form of a male voice choir who are in full song most Monday evenings.

Denis and Julie Churchill successfully run this Devenish owned inn serving Flowers I.P.A., Cornish Original and a guest ale straight from the barrel.

A printed menu is supplemented by a range of daily changing dishes which are chalked up on a blackboard beside the bar. Mostly all the food is home-cooked and includes a choice of soups, ham and cheddar ploughmans, ham, egg and chips, a range of omelettes, lasagne, plaice fillets and steaks. The specials board may offer ham, courgette, onion and pasta bake, prawn, tuna and pasta bake, steak and vegetable pie and pan-fried rainbow trout. There is also a good choice of vegetarian dishes. Food is served between 12 noon and 2 p.m. and 7 p.m. till 9 p.m.

Children are welcome in the rooms away from the bar if supervised and their is no objection to dogs.

Weekday opening times are from 11 a.m. till 2.30 p.m. and 6 p.m till 11 p.m.
Telephone: (0736) 740574.

Village is situated on the B3309, ½ mile off the A30, 3½ miles north east of Penzance.

Approx. distance of walk: 3½ miles. O.S. Map No. 203 SW 505/330.

There is a small parking area in front of the pub.

A short undulating walk along well defined paths through woodland and across meadowland with magnificient views across St. Mounts Bay and St. Michael's Mount.

1. From the pub go up the steps into the graveyard, bear right then left around the church, pass through a metal gate turning right onto a trackway. This shortly becomes a pathway to a stone stile, then proceed downhill taking the centre path through the woodland into the valley. Cross over a tiny brook and stile at the bottom and head uphill across lush meadowland towards a house to another stile and shortly turn left onto a country lane. After a short distance turn right across a stone stile to follow the waymarked path along the left hand edge of the field with open rural views to a further stone stile then bear diagonally left across a field on a defined path gradually descending the valley side. In the corner go over the stile, pass through an old woodland then walk briefly beside a brook before crossing a small footbridge to a small gate on the right.
2. Bear diagonally left uphill, cross a stone stile beside a gate, keep to the left hand edge of the field with fine views back towards St. Michael's Mount and soon turn left onto a metalled lane. Follow the lane around the sharp left hand corner then shortly turn left into Boskennel Farm and keep to the signed path between two barns and through a metal gate ahead. Bear left around the main barn following the track down onto a flattened soil area, bear right onto a narrow path (can be overgrown) downhill into woodland. Cross a stile, bear left past a water pump, cross the footbridge over the brook and proceed uphill to climb a tricky wall stile ahead. Bear right uphill, through a gate at the top of the field, keep to the right hand edge of the next field to a stile in the corner. Cross this and the stile ahead on the left then turn left along a metalled driveway to a country lane.
3. Go across the lane onto a waymarked track downhill past a cottage on the left before bearing left at the bottom onto a narrow path across a brook, through a metal swing gate and along the well defined route across a field keeping to the left of the walled hedge ahead. Go up six stone steps on the right, turn left into an open field and

bear diagonally right towards the stone buildings ahead. Cross a stone stile to follow the path to the rear of the cottages to another stile and cross the road ahead onto an arrowed path through the bottom of a garden.
4. Go across the field ahead to a stone stile with open views across Mounts Bay to the left, then keep to the right hand edge of a large field, cross a stile in the hedge on the right and keep ahead on a track into another field. Follow the right hand hedge, cross a stone stile in the far corner, pass through a small thicket, cross another stile turning left along the field edge before crossing a stile hidden in the hedge onto a lane. Turn left, remaining on the lane to a wall stile just beyond the first house passed on the right. Keep to the right hand edge before bearing off left to cross a stile in the left hand corner. Proceed ahead, cross a stone stile in the corner, follow the path along the right hand edge to cross a stile near a house and turn along the road back to the church and pub.

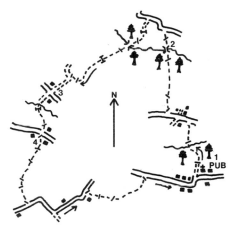

The Heron Inn, Malpas

The Heron was built in 1840 and was known as the Park Hotel until 1945 when it became a pub and re-named after the large heronry that once existed among Woodbury trees across the Truro River. The inn is very popular in summer months for its glorious sunny-slate-paved front terrace which has lovely views over the Truro and Tresillian Rivers and their heavily wooded riverbanks. Inside, the long, comfortable rectangular bar has a fine collection of late 19th century photographs of Truro and the surrounding countryside, various brasses, plates and bric-a-brac, and numerous photographs and trophies relating to the landlords hobby of Sporting Car Trials. The carpeted bar is furnished with red plush upholstered wall seats and stools and modern dark wood tables. A smaller adjoining games room has a pool table.

The inn is a St. Austell pub well run by Calvin and Anne Kneebone. Two real ales are served on hand pump, Hicks Special and Tinners Ale.

Good bar food includes generously filled sandwiches, especially the local crab, a turkey club sandwich which is served with chips, ploughmans, pork sâté, marinated chicken wings, steak and kidney pie, liver and bacon kebabs, ham, egg and chips, cauliflower cheese and a range of basket meals. Also available are a mixed grill, turkey Roquefort, steaks and a range of daily specials which may include seafood lasagne, chicken masala and trout. Apple pie and chocolate fudge cake are usually on the sweet list. During the summer there is a barbeque every Thursday, Friday and Saturday nights. There is a separate children's menu. Food is served seven days a week between 12 noon and 2 p.m. and from 6.30 p.m. till 9.30 p.m.

Families are welcome but dogs are not allowed inside the pub.

Weekday opening times are from 11 a.m. till 3 p.m. and from 6 p.m. till 11 p.m. Telephone: (0872) 72773.

Village lies 2 miles south east of Truro signed from the main roundabout on the A39.

Approx. distance of walk: 3½ miles, O.S. Map No. 204 SW 843/426.

Parking is difficult, the only space available is along the lane in the village. It is advisable to arrive early for the walk, especially in summer.

A delightful walk along the banks of the Truro and Tresillian Rivers incorporating the peaceful hamlet of St. Clement, old tracks and farmland paths. Easy going for most of the way, one of the tracks can be very muddy in wet weather.

1. Leave the pub and turn left along the lane passing the small quay area on the right. Shortly, follow the waymarked footpath off to the right, keeping left along a driveway. Take the path to the left of the house, pass through a wooden swing gate into woodland. Cross a plank bridge over a small brook, turn right and follow the footpath "Denas Road" beside the brook to the river's edge. Climb a stile and remain on the well defined path through coniferous woodland along the banks of River Tresillian. Soon leave the wood via a stile, then keep to the right hand edge along the river bank and climb two more stiles to re-enter the wood. Follow the yellow arrows and eventually join a lane beside a small quay in the hamlet of St. Clements.

2. Turn left, uphill passing the vicarage and the church on the right. Proceed uphill, disregard the first footpath on the left to "Malpas" and take the second waymarked path in front of the village hall. Keep right onto an established path uphill to a small wooden gate and head straight across the

field keeping to the left of the telegraph poles to a small metal gate. Follow the track to a lane, turn left then immediately right (yellow arrow) onto an old trackway. Proceed downhill keeping ahead at the junction of paths to cross a wooden footbridge over a brook in the valley bottom. This stretch of path can be extremely muddy after rain.

3. Head uphill, bear left onto a farm track and shortly turn left again onto a concrete drive. Pass in front of a black barn and follow the signed pathway ahead through a wooden gate. Keep to the right hand edge of the field, downhill with views across Truro River. Cross a stile hidden in the hedge in the corner and follow the narrow path beside houses, downhill to a lane. Cross over, turn left and walk through Boscawen Park shortly to pass the cricket ground. Bear right along a short concrete quay, climb the wooden steps at the end and turn right onto a narrow path which runs parallel to the road along the wooded river bank. Rejoin the road on the edge of Malpas village and follow it back to the inn.

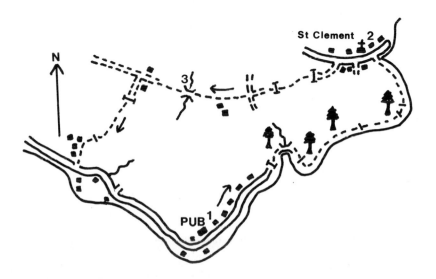

New Inn, Manaccan

The thatched, cottage-like New Inn is situated in the heart of this peaceful and totally unspoilt village which escapes the throng of visitors that crowd the coastal areas nearby. This relaxed and traditional atmosphere pervades throughout this homely inn although its age isn't really clear. It is known to date back to Cromwellian times as it was specifically made out of bounds to soldiers during the Civil War. The interior remains as it did a hundred years or so ago, rustic and traditional with boarded walls and exposed ceilings. The double-roomed bar is furnished with a mix of simple tables and chairs, built-in wall settles and old rugs on the stone floor. A large inglenook has a table and a couple of chairs within it. The walls are adorned with a range of oil paintings, some of which are for sale. There is a large shrub-filled garden to the rear with peaceful rural views and two benches out the front.

The New Inn is owned by Devenish and run by licensee Patrick Cullinan who aims to keep the rustic charm and character that makes this pub so special. Marstons Pedigree and Cornish Original are well conditioned and drawn straight from the barrel on a rack behind the bar. There is also a fine selection of wines to choose from.

A short blackboard menu offers excellent home-cooked dishes beginning with asparagus soup or maybe chilled pea and mint soup, local crab pâté, chicken liver pate or smoked salmon. Main dishes may include macaroni Bolognese, chicken fricassee with pasta, home-baked ham in cider, sirloin steak and superb fresh fish such as John Dory, plaice, brill and salmon. Oysters and lobster can be ordered if 24 hours notice is given. Good puddings come with clotted cream; apple pie, treacle tart, chocolate roulade and sticky toffee pudding. Sandwiches and a few lighter dishes are available at lunchtimes when food is served between 12 noon and 2.30 p.m., evening food is served from 6.30 p.m. till 9.30 p.m.

Children and well behaved dogs are very welcome inside the pub.

Weekday opening times are from 11 a.m. till 3 p.m. and 6 p.m. till 11 p.m.

Telephone: (032623) 323.

Take the A3083 from Helston towards the Lizard turning left onto the B3293 for Coverack. Turn left for Newtown St. Martin and follow signs for Manaccan and Helford.

Approx. distance of walk: 5 miles. O.S. Map No. 204 SW 763/250.

Parking is limited at the pub. It is best to park up the lane or in front of the church.

An undulating scenic walk across easy going farmland paths and tracks, returning along a peaceful country lane.

1. Leave the New Inn and turn left uphill for a short distance before bearing right beside the "old well" onto a narrow tarmac pathway uphill in front of some cottages to the Post Office. Turn right onto a lane which soon bears left round the churchyard and turn right onto an unmetalled lane opposite a churchyard gate. After 100 yards bear right along a pathway beside a graveyard signed "Carne", go downhill, across a stone stile with fine views to the right over fields back to the pub and down into a wooded valley. Keep to the right-hand edge of the field across another stile and field to a stile in the corner where the path now descends into a wooded valley. At the bottom cross the footbridge over the brook, turn left onto a quiet lane which shortly passes alongside a picturesque wooded creek into the tiny hamlet of Carne.

2. Remain on the lane, uphill out of Carne and take the waymarked path on the right over a stile, soon to emerge onto a well defined path uphill across an open field. Cross the stile in the hedge, keep to the left-hand edge of the next field to the stile beside a metal gate and proceed ahead along a cobbled lane. Pass through a metal gate, turn left and enter Treworthack farmyard, bearing right then left through the yard.

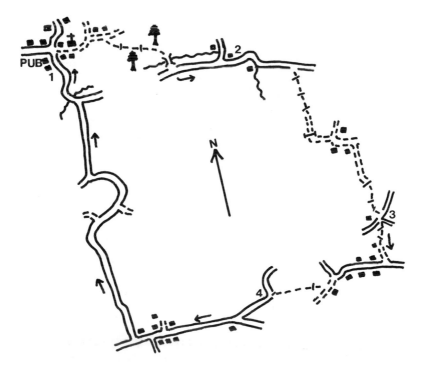

Turn right onto a signed trackway beyond the second barn downhill into a field, then follow the waymarked path uphill to a stile in the hedge. Now follow the orange arrows on the stiles across three fields joining a country lane near a house.

3. Turn right, then after thirty yards bear off left onto a narrow grassy path between two flower-filled hedges in summer months. At the end of this path cross a wall stile on the left and bear right downhill along the edge of the field towards a cottage visible in the trees. Go over another wall stile and soon pass the cottage on the right to join its driveway, following it out to a lane. Turn right through the hamlet of Tregarne and where the lane bears right uphill turn left onto an old cobbled lane. On reaching a whitewashed stone cottage bear right onto a grassy path (can be overgrown) between hedges. Cross a wall stile at the end with beautiful open rural views and bear right across a field towards a disintegrated wall. Go into the next field keeping left along the wall to a gate and wall stile in the corner.

4. Turn left along a narrow lane, bear right at the junction of lanes ahead and shortly enter the hamlet of Tregowris. Pass through the hamlet, turn right at the next junction onto another peaceful narrow lane and remain on it for $1\frac{1}{4}$ miles with scenic views across rolling Cornish countryside. Descend a steep hill to a T-junction and turn left uphill back into Manaccan and the pub.

A Riverside Path, Metherell

The Carpenters Arms, Metherell

This delightful 15th century inn is tucked away in the village centre, amidst a web of narrow lanes and close to the River Tamar and the magnificent Tudor manor house of Cotehele (National Trust). The pub was built by – and housed – the carpenters who were constructing Cotehele Manor. The public bar is the original building and is full of character and charm with heavy beams, a fine old slate floor, exposed stone walls adorned with various brasses, comfortable window bench seating and a mix of other tables and chairs. The more recently added lounge bar is surprisingly large and provides a good dining area. It is furnished with dark wood "pub" tables, wheel-backed chairs, settles and some modern pine furniture. A few old photographs and general nick-nacks decorate the stone walls. The front terrace is popular on fine summer days. Picnic benches and wooden tables are set among tubs of plants and hanging baskets, close to the old well.

The pub is a free house, very well run by the owners Douglas and Jill Brace. In summer months four real ales are served such as Bass, Wadworth 6X, and Flowers Original, with a guest beer usually served straight from the cask. In winter months only one or two ales are kept.

A comprehensive menu is supplemented with a few daily specials and is available seven days a week from 12 noon till 1.45 p.m. and 7 p.m. till 9.30 p.m. The printed menu has a wide range of dishes from sandwiches and jacket potatoes to good value main courses – cottage pie, chicken curry, fish and prawn pie, fresh trout with almonds, chicken and ham pie, beef bourgnignon, fillet of pork, turkey casserole with vegetables and herb dumplings, liver and bacon casserole and various salads and omelettes. Vegetarian dishes are well featured with hot and spicy chilli beans, Chinese bean casserole and ratatouille. Puddings include treacle sponge and Carpenter's spicy pudding. Children have their own menu.

Weekday opening times are from 12 noon (11.30 a.m. in summer) till 2.30 p.m. (3 p.m. on Saturday) and 7 p.m. (6.30 p.m. in summer) till 11 p.m.

Children are welcome in the dining area and there is no objection to dogs in the bars.

Telephone: (0579) 50242.

The village is signposted from the A390 at St. Ann's Chapel, just west of Gunnislake.

Approx. distance of walk: 4½ miles. O.S. Map No. 201 SX 409/694.

Parking is difficult, there are spaces for about eight cars at the inn.

This is a delightful family walk, predominantly through peaceful National Trust woodland along the edge of the River Tamar, past Cotehele Mill Quay and the restored Tamar sailing barge "The Shamrock" and close to the superb Tudor manor of Cotehele. It was the home of the Edgcumbe family for centuries and contains original furniture, armour and needlework. Attractive terraced gardens.

1. From the pub turn right up to a T-junction in the village and turn left. Pass the farm shop and church and follow the narrow lane through the village. At the end of the houses at a right hand bend pass through a metal gate on your left. Follow the left hand hedge of an arable field with glorious views across rolling countryside. This defined grassy path soon heads downhill towards a coniferous plantation in the valley. Cross a wooden fence and proceed downhill along the edge of another field to a stile in the corner. A narrow path leads you down to a quiet country lane and a stream. Turn left along a lane to a T-junction.

2. Turn left and follow the narrow lane uphill to where a lane bears off to your right, signed Cotehele. Turn right here and remain on this lane until you reach Elbow Cottage on the left. Turn right through a white gate onto an arrowed path – signed Cotehele Mill and Quay – that zig-zags

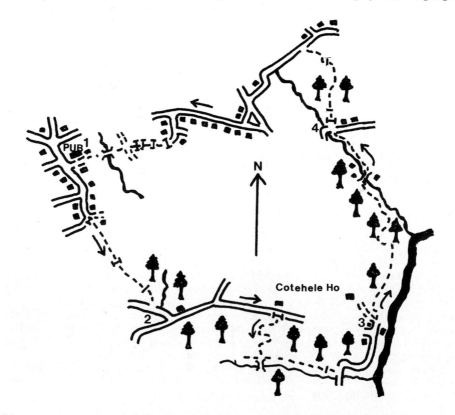

downhill through the woodland (NT) into the valley. Keep ahead on merging with the valley bottom path. If you wish to visit Cotehele Mill, bear right over the river for the footpath to the Mill. Follow the peaceful established riverside path through the mainly beech, oak and larch woodland. Pass to the side of a gate and join a lane beside a bridge. Keep ahead towards the Quay, with views across the Tamar valley. Shortly, pass the Maritime Museum, The Shamrock barge and the National Trust tearoom on the Quay and enter the car park.

3. Bear left onto a woodland path, waymarked Danescombe and Calstock. Soon enjoy river views from this delightful path. Pass an old chapel, the wide woodland path gradually winds its way uphill. Pass a small gate which allows access to the magnificent manor and lovely gardens of Cotehele – well worth a visit – and keep right at the next junction of paths. Descend into Danescombe Valley and bear left on reaching a trackway to follow the fast flowing stream uphill. Gradually ascend, pass a couple of cottages (NT), cross over the brook and remain on the track passing an old mill on your left. Eventually, emerge out onto a lane and turn left. Cross the river, then bear off right onto a footpath signed Todsworthy.

4. Go through a wooden gate and bear right onto a footpath, just below a green-painted cottage. Proceed uphill beside the river passing a few sheds to a stile. Shortly, cross another stile into a field and follow the right hand hedge along the base of the hill. The defined grassy path gradually curves left uphill to a lane. Turn left and follow this to a T-junction. Turn left towards Norris Green, then turn right at the next junction, signed Metherell. Keep right and soon turn left along Nicholas Meadow, then take the first right downhill into a cul-de-sac to a footpath in the right hand corner, waymarked Lower Metherell. Pass through two swing gates and keep right along the edge of a crop field to a wooden gate. Bear right along what can be a very muddy track to a gate beside a house called Brooklands. Follow the path downhill, cross a brook and enter Lower Metherell and proceed ahead along the lane, back to the pub.

A River Bridge near Cotehele House

The Miners Arms, Mithian

The ancient Miners Arms was built in 1557 and nestles in the tiny picturesque village of Mithian only minutes away from the bustling beaches along the north coast. Unspoilt character and charm are immediately evident as you cross the cobbled courtyard and enter the flagged stone hall that leads to the atmospheric small rooms. The main bar has bulging squint walls, a low plank and beam ceiling, wood block floor, an open log fire and is furnished with cushioned wall seats and bar stools. The cosy lounge has genuine Elizabethan friezes decorating its low ceiling, half wood panelled walls and shelves full of books, old bottles and interesting ornaments. A further lounge area has padded wall seats and the small dining room upstairs is also simply furnished. The stone-built cellar lounge is the children's room and has doors opening out into the sheltered back garden. Two other interesting historical features are the Penance cupboard which at one time had a beautifully carved mahogany seat and it is said a secret stone lined passage ran underground to the manor house across the road.

The inn is owned by the Cornish brewery and successfully run by David and Dilys Charnock. Marstons Pedigree and Boddingtons Bitter are the regular real ales served by hand pump.

Popular home-cooked bar food is served daily between 12 noon and 2 p.m. and from 6.30 p.m. till 10 p.m. The printed menu is supplemented by daily blackboard specials. Begin with a choice of crab bake, watercress soup, pork and chicken liver pâté or a variety of garlic breads and progress to hearty main dishes such as steak and kidney pie, beef curry, Chinese duck, pork spare ribs, lasagne, fish pie and prawn, crab or ham salad. Ploughmans and sandwiches are also available. Puddings include bread and butter pudding and toffee apple fudge cake. Children have their own menu.

Weekday opening times are from 12 noon till 3 p.m. and from 6 p.m. till 11 p.m.

Children are welcome away from the bar and there is no objection to dogs.

Telephone: (087255) 2375.

Village is situated between the B3284 and B3285 two miles east of St. Agnes.

Approx. distance walk: 4½ miles. O.S. Map No. 204 SW 744/506.

The pub has a large car park.

An enjoyable easy going walk along peaceful valley pathways and quiet narrow lanes.

1. From the pub turn left and follow the lane downhill into the valley. Near the bottom turn left onto the signed footpath towards "Perrancombe" and proceed through woodland on a well defined path parallel with the stream. Cross a stile into lush meadowland and keep to the valley bottom path to another stile. Climb this and cross the meadow ahead keeping to the left of the barn towards a wall stile beside a gate. Turn right onto a narrow lane, then shortly bear left at a junction of lanes to follow a lane along the valley side. Pass Blowing House Mill on the right then turn left uphill onto the waymarked trackway "Trevellas Post Office".

2. Enter the driveway of a house and keep to the right of the house (signed), climbing some stone steps onto a narrow, well defined pathway between hedges. Gradually ascend with open rural views all round and bear left on joining a metalled lane. The lane soon gives way to a rough track, keep right at the next junction, then shortly, turn right beside a house and proceed uphill bearing left at the top to join the B3285.

3. Turn left then in a short distance bear off right onto a lane towards "Cross Combe". Keep right at the next junction with views across to St. Agnes and old mine workings. Pass Trevellas Manor farm then at the next left hand bend go straight on along a track in front of a house to join a well established path which soon descends into Trevellas Combe. Cross a concrete footbridge over a small brook, bear left uphill, then bear left again onto a grassy path along the valley bottom.

4. Cross a busy B-road and follow the waymarked path "Wheal Butson" through this beautiful valley. Cross the stream and proceed uphill then along the edge of a field behind a large house. On reaching its driveway bear left uphill under the bridge adjoining the viaduct and turn left onto a lane. At the junction ahead turn right and remain on the lane turning left at the T-junction signed "Mithian". Follow this lane downhill into the village back to the pub.

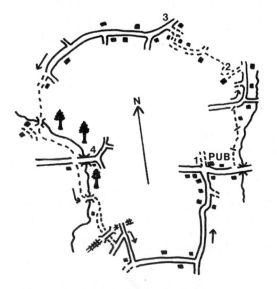

The Bush Inn, Morwenstow

This delightful ancient country inn is set in the isolated cliff-top hamlet of Crosstown and is reputed to be one of the oldest pubs in Britain. It was once a monastic resting house on the pilgrim route between Spain and Wales and parts of the building date back to 950 when it was a hermits cell. There is also a Celtic piscina carved from serpeintine stone set in one wall by the bar. It is unspoilt and traditional – a real gem – the two bars being music and electronic game free, its appeal and atmosphere being created in the main bar by the heavy flagged stone floor, the ancient built-in settles and the old stone fireplaces. A snug area is furnished with various antique and rustic pieces of furniture and local paintings along with a wooden propeller from the plane that Amy Johnson used on her inaugural flight to Australia. An upper bar – open at busy times – is decorated with miners lamps, casks, funnels, plates and clocks. For fine weather imbibing there is a sheltered courtyard with picnic benches and a peaceful garden.

The pub is a free house serving excellent St. Austell Hicks Special plus in winter months a winter brew such as Exmoor Beast and regular guest beers in the summer months – Bass, Wadworth 6X and possibly Cotleigh Old Buzzard.

A short lunchtime menu offers simple, yet hearty pub fare such as a thick warming soup, beef stew, fish pie, steak and kidney pie, chicken and ham pie, lasagne and when available fresh local crab. Generously filled sandwiches, various ploughmans with home-made pickle and locally made pasties are usually on offer as well. Sweets may include spotted dick. Food is only served at lunchtimes, except Sunday, between 12 noon and 2.30 p.m.

Both children and dogs are not allowed in the pub.

Weekday opening times are from 12 noon till 3 p.m. and from 7 p.m. till 11 p.m., with the usual Sunday hours. From October through to January the pub is closed all day Monday.

Telephone: (028883) 242.

The village is signposted off the A39, north of Bude.

Approx. distance of walk 4½ miles. O.S. Map No. 190 SS 208/151.

It is possible to park on the grassy area outside the pub, alternatively you can park down the lane opposite the church.

An exhilarating and quite strenuous high cliff walk, affording superb coastal views and across to Lundy Island, returning through farmland. Morwenstow is Cornwall's most northerly parish and is a fascinating place, best known for its eccentric vicar and poet Robert John Hawker. From 1834 he spent 40 years serving a mixed multitude of smugglers, wreckers and dissenters.

1. From the pub follow the lane left down to the church of St. Morwenna, tucked in a dell and looking out to sea. It has magnificent Norman carvings on its porch and a splendid interior. The vicarage below is where Hawker lived and has unusual chimneys based on two Oxford colleges, three Cornish church towers and the tombstone of Hawker's mother. The churchyard contains the graves of drowned sailors, retrieved by Hawker from wrecks in order to give them a Christian burial. On leaving the church follow the path by the car park towards Vicarage Cliff, through a couple of fields beside a wall to your left. At the cliff edge, join the coastal footpath. A short detour can be made by turning left to visit Hawker's Hut – a cliff-top retreat where he wrote, meditated and looked out for wrecks. Our route heads north along the coast path.

2. Follow the grass cliff edge, then a shaley path downhill into a deep combe and a footbridge across the stream. A good place to see Kestrels and Ravens. Climb steeply out of the combe with views back to Morwenstow church. At the top – Henna Cliff – follow yellow cliff arrow along the edge of pastureland. Superb views south beyond Bude and north to Lundy and Hartland. The coast path begins to traverse very rural, unspoilt region of Devon and Cornwall, with dramatic cliffs and folded rock strata. Follow acorn symbols and yellow arrows into a couple of combes with footbridges. Ascend steeply from the last combe via wooden steps out onto Marsland Cliff and the welcome sight of a bench. Gradually descend into Marsland Mouth.

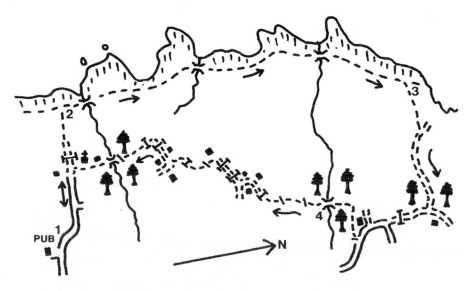

3. On reaching a wooden post turn right to follow a gently rising path heading inland across the bramble and bracken covered hillside. Join a wide stony track and follow this gradually uphill through scrub and trees to another track and house. Turn right uphill passing "Little Marsland" and go through a gate, shortly reaching a lane. Follow the arrow pointing you right along the lane and pass Marsland Manor. In a little way cross a stile on the right, keep ahead along a hedge following yellow arrow directing you through the hedge and join an old pathway that heads downhill into the wooded combe.

4. Cross two wooden footbridges, head uphill with yellow arrow to a stile on the woodland edge. Go across a field to a stone stile in hedgerow, then bear half-left on a defined path to a wooden gate. Follow the arrow directing you towards Cornakey farm ahead. A grass, then muddy track bears right towards the farmhouse. Pass through the farmyard the route arrowed left on the wall ahead directing you up the metalled farm drive. At a left hand bend bear right through a wooden gate onto a track, signed to Yeolmouth. Pass to the left of Yeolmouth Cottage to a wooden gate and head towards another house, soon to bear left to a stile. Go over, follow the right hand hedge, pass through a gateway, then at post with arrow follow a concrete drive to Westcott farm. Bear right in front of the farmhouse, following the track between barns (muddy) to a wooden gate. Turn left, pass through another gate and head downhill towards Morwenstow church. Enter woodland on a muddy path and cross a stile and old stone bridge. Proceed uphill passing the vicarage and continue uphill through the churchyard to the car park. Turn left along the lane back to the pub.

The Coastal Path, Morwenstow

A Deep Coombe, Morwenstow

Wild Flowers Line a Path on the Walk from Mousehole

The Ship Inn, Mousehole

Mousehole or "Mouzell" to the locals is one of Cornwall's most ancient ports. Tiers of pretty cottages, narrow alleyways and flowery courtyards surround the tiny picturesque harbour where 100 years ago over 400 fishing vessels would be packed between its walls. Pride of place on the harbour goes to the Ship Inn, a 400 year old stone hostelry which retains much of its charm and character. The rustic unspoilt main bar has low black beams and panelling, flagged granite floors, open log fires, built-in wooden wall benches, deep window seats and stools around low tables. A nautical theme runs throughout the pub with various artefacts such as a sailor's ropework display, a propellor and numerous photographs of local shipwrecks including the Torry Canyon. Upstairs there is a sheltered terrace with tables and chairs looking out over the village rooftops. Tom Bawcocks' Eve is celebrated in the pub every 23 December and recalls the time when a local fisherman saved the local people from famine by sailing out in a storm and returning with a large catch of seven sorts of fish. A special dish, "Starry-gazy pie" is still baked and eaten in his honour.

It is a St. Austell pub well run by Michael and Tracy Maddern. Three well kept real ales are drawn from the cellar, Hicks Special, Tinners Ale and Bosun's Bitter.

Most of the food is home-made and the printed menu offers crab chowder, stuffed aubergines and a pâté among the starters followed by peppered steaks, lamb kebabs, baked fish gratin, seafood platter or tagliatelle with a vegetable sauce. Puddings may include blackcurrent cheesecake. At lunchtime simpler bar snacks range from chilli and lasagne to sandwiches and salads with excellent fresh crab. Bar food is served 12 noon till 2.30 pm and 6 pm till 9 pm. There is also a restaurant.

Weekday opening times are from 11 a.m. till 11 p.m. between Easter and October, otherwise 11 a.m. till 3 p.m. and 6 p.m. till 11 p.m.

There is an area set aside for families and dogs are allowed in the pub.

The inn has three letting ensuite bedrooms.

Telephone: (0736) 731234.

The village is situated off the B3315 south west of Penzance.

Approx. distance of walk: 4 miles. O.S. Map No. 203 SW 470/263.

Park in either the harbour car park or in the pay and display car park at the edge of the village.

An undulating scenic cliff walk with some tricky descents through scrubland to the peaceful Lamorna Cove which once exported high quality granite from its tiny harbour. The return route crosses fields and passes through old farmsteads.

1. From the Ship turn right away from the harbour and follow the narrow street through the village soon to ascend steeply after passing the Wesleyian Chapel. Take time on this hill to admire the view across Mousehole to St. Michael's Mount. Where the road turns right bear off left onto the coast path signed 'Lamorna', at first a fine green lane abundant with wild flowers in early summer then a narrow path which zig-zags through scrubland across the shelving cliff.

2. Pass through "Kemyel Crease Nature Reserve" a small woodland rich in flora and fauna onto grassland before ascending the cliffside. Gradually descend on a boulder-strewn path into Lamorna Cove. Before reaching the cottages and stream turn right onto a path leading inland past the old quarries to Kemyel Wartha farm.

3. Bear right behind the farm buildings to a stile and signed footpath. Keep to the left-hand edge of the first field, straight across the second then head towards the right of the farm buildings that are in view. Cross a stile into Kemyel Crease farm, remain on the track beyond the farm taking the way-marked path to the right soon to cross a stile and stone bridge. The path crosses a short stretch of moorland before joining a track through the farmyard of Kemyel Drea.

4. At the end of a barn cross a stone stile on the right, head downhill across three fields then keep left where the path forks shortly to cross a stone stile and a lane into Raginnis farm. Keep right through the farmyard, cross a wall stile on the right and head downhill across four fields via stone stiles with Mousehole coming into view. Drop down a few steps, cross a track then go down a steep path with a stream on the left back down into the village. Walk along the narrow back streets to the harbour and the pub.

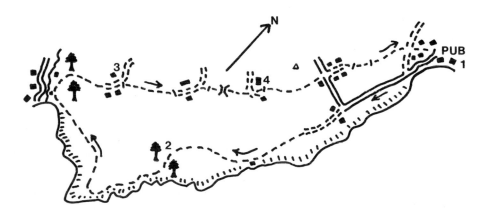

The Shipwrights Arms, Padstow

The Shipwrights Arms enjoys a splendid position overlooking the busy harbour in this attractive medieval town, which has remained relatively unspoilt, despite being a very popular holiday destination. The pub, as its name implies used to be a boat building warehouse at the time when Padstow was an important trading port, but the formation of the Doom Bar sandbank across the mouth of the estuary prevented large vessels using the harbour. Today, as a pub it serves the town's growing industry – tourism – refreshing visitors who stroll around the interesting quay. Inside, the large bar has a low beamed ceiling, strung with a furled-up sail, lifebelts, oars and numerous other bits of nautical bric-a-brac. Slate floors, an old brick fireplace, part wood panelled walls, cushioned wall bench seating and various old photographs of bygone Padstow create a good atmosphere in this lively establishment. A spiral staircase leads to the attractive restaurant which has fine harbour views. Tables and chairs outside on a paved area are the most sought after seats on fine summer days. There is also a beer terrace to the rear.

The pub is owned by the St. Austell brewery, dispensing well conditioned Hicks Special and Tinners Ale.

A large blackboard advertises the varied menu which can be sampled between 12 noon and 2 p.m. and from 7 p.m. till 9 p.m. As well as a good range of sandwiches and salads on offer there are filled jacket potatoes – cheese, cheese and ham, prawn and fresh local crab for example. Hot dishes include plaice or cod and chips, spicy beef and bean casserole, half fresh lobster and various steaks.

Children are very welcome inside.

Winter weekday opening times are from 11 a.m. till 3 p.m and 6.30 p.m. till 11 p.m. In summer months the pub is open all day, from 11 a.m. till 11 p.m.

Telephone: (0841) 532451.

Padstow lies near the mouth of the River Camel on the A389, north west of Wadebridge.

Approx. distance of walk: 5 miles. O.S. Map No. 200 SW 917/753.

It is best to park at one of the public car parks on the edge of the town and walk to the harbour.

A delightful fairly easy going walk along sheltered estuary paths, across dramatic cliffs and returning across peaceful farmland paths. Open coastal views can be enjoyed from Stepper Point.

1. Leave the Shipwrights and turn left away from the harbour. Follow the coast path sign uphill past the crazy golf hut – good views back across the harbour – and enter Chapelstile Field. Pass some new flats and follow the tarmac path gradually uphill across the recreation area, with views over the estuary to the dunes beyond Rock. Go past the memorial cross, through a metal swing gate and enjoy the scene ahead to Padstow Bay. The path becomes gravelly and well established, soon curving left into St. George's Cove. Pass round Gun Point where the path becomes narrow and grassy along the edge of arable land. Cross a few stone stiles, the coast path leading you into Harbour Cove. On reaching a sandy track, turn right, then left with the arrow to cross a footbridge. Shortly climb a stile and drop down through a wooded marshy area, following yellow arrows across a duckboard and over a trackway.

2. Remain on the established route to Hawkers Cove and the site of the old lifeboat station and coastguard cottages. At a metalled lane turn right, pass in front of a house and follow coast path sign right, around the rear of the cottages. Go through a wooden swing gate and begin the gradual climb up to Stepper Point – delightful vistas over the estuary and back, on a clear day to Bodmin Moor. At the Point cross the stile and follow the cliff path to a stone beacon – built to aid navigation into the port. Where the path splits take the lower grassy path right, cross a stile and pass round Pepper and Butter Holes with fine cliff scenery to a wooden swing gate. A good level stretch of a cliff path leads you to a stile. Leave the coast path, turning left with the white arrow, along the edge of a field to a stile and lane. Turn right and follow the lane into the hamlet of Crugmeer.

3. Turn left in the hamlet by the post box along a lane, passing a farm on the left and soon take the waymarked footpath across a stile on the right. A well defined path crosses seven fields and as many stiles to a stile preceding a metalled lane. Turn right and follow the quiet lane downhill, under an arch and pass in front of a magnificent Elizabethan Manor – Prideaux Place (open in summer). Now on the outskirts of Padstow, turn left and follow the road back down into the centre of the town and the harbour.

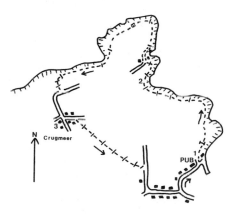

The sketch maps in this book are not necessarily to scale but have been drawn to show the maximum amount of detail.

The Victoria Inn, Perranuthnoe

Situated on a peaceful lane leading up to the church, the attractive Victoria Inn was built to accomodate the masons who extended the church in the 15th century and has since been officially described as safe house for the clergy. The pretty pink-washed stone exterior is adorned with hanging baskets and from the few benches beside the flowerbeds across the lane there is a good view out across the fields to the sea. The inn sign shows a very young Queen Victoria. There is a warm welcome to all who enter this friendly pub especially families. The large L-shaped bar has a beamed ceiling and some of the walls have been stripped back to stone. Furnished with settles and a mix of chairs around polished wooden tables, the bar is comfortable and a snug alcove is ideal for intimate dining. Local coastal and wreck photographs and various maritime memorabilia decorate the bar. There is a more modern and spacious family area with high-backed settles, juke box and various pub games. A sheltered walled garden has some picnic benches and is popular in summer for its regular barbeque.

The pub is owned by Ushers and serves three well conditioned real ales on hand pump – Courage Directors, John Smiths Yorkshire Bitter and Ushers Best Bitter.

The cooking here is reliable, freshly prepared daily specials supplementing the printed menu. Favourites include chicken and ham pie, chilli, chicken curry, excellent steaks and a variety of filled jacket potatoes – ham, cheese, prawn and coleslaw to name but a few. A range of sandwiches and salads are available as well as vegetarian dishes such as nut rissoles in pepper sauce, A short selection of sweets include sticky toffee pudding and chocolate fudge cake. Children have their own menu. Food is served daily from 12 noon till 2 p.m. and from 6.30 p.m. till 9.30 p.m.

Children are welcome so too are dogs.

Weekday opening times are from 12 noon till 3 p.m. and from 6.30 p.m. till 11 p.m.

The inn has two letting bedrooms.

Telephone: (0736) 710309

Village is signposted off A394 Penzance to Helston road.

Approx. distance of walk: 4½ miles. O.S. Map No. 203 SW 539/296.

The inn has a small car park and there is a public car park near the beach (charge).

A scenic coast path walk with views to St. Michael's Mount returning along rural tracks and paths. Undulating, yet easy going underfoot. A good family ramble.

1. Leaving the Victoria Inn turn right and follow the lane through the village to the beach car park. Walk south-east along the lane that flanks the lower end of the car park, waymarked "coast path". Bear right in front of "Blue Burrow" cottage following the coast path signs down to the cliff edge with views across to the Land's End peninsula and Penzance. The path from here is easy going keeping to the edges of fields across the gently shelving cliffs. Shortly, St. Michael's Mount will come into view as the path rounds Trevean Cove. Pass below Acton Castle – built by Admiral Stackhouse in 1775 as a base for his research into seaweeds – away to the left and head towards Cudden Point. Cross gorse and scrub covered cliffs which are alive with birdlife. Climb a stile onto NT land and climb steeply up to the headland from which the expanse of the Lizard can be viewed.

2. The path undulates around a few coves, from Piskies Cove into Bessy's Cove and the deep inlet known as Prussia Cove which is named after the famous 18th century smuggler John Carter who styled himself after Frederick the Great of Prussia. Pass an old thatched fishermans shed on the cliff edge and bear left towards the houses at the head of the cove. Pass a thatched cottage and bear right along a gravel track uphill to a gate beside a metalled drive and follow a pathway parallel to the drive downhill to another gravel track. Keep left, shortly to pass between two fine houses with a turning circle for cars. The track passes in front of a row of cottages to a gate, pass to one side and soon where the coast path divides, bear left inland onto a narrow path uphill. Emerge from the thicket onto a grass area and keep right of the building ahead onto a stony pathway. Pass to the side of a wooden

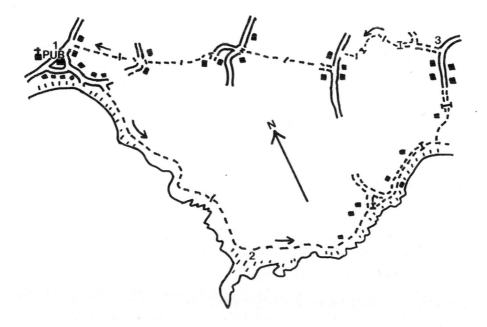

gate remaining on the defined hedged path which soon gives way to a wide track before becoming a metalled lane in the hamlet of Kenneggy.

3. Beyond the hamlet where the lane bears right take the trackway to the left near the entrance to "Sunny Vale Farm". Follow this green lane downhill, keeping left where the track divides and soon pass through a metal gate. Look out for a stone wall stile on the right, climb this and turn left along the edge of the field to a wooden gate. Cross the stepping stones in the brook ahead, keep left over a stone stile then turn right along a defined path to another gate and soon join a lane. Follow the lane left, uphill to a way-marked path on the right opposite "Rosudgeon Farm". Cross a wall stile flanking a metal gate and keep left through the field to another wall stile in the left-hand corner.

Follow the right-hand edge of the next field which affords fine views to the Land's End peninsula. Keep to the right of a garage to a wooden gate and cross a lane following the arrowed route along a gravel track. Where this turns left by a building, bear right onto grass then immediately turn right again across a stile into a field. Bear half-left across the pasture to a stone stile, keep to the right-hand edge of the next field with stunning views across Mounts Bay. Proceed downhill towards "Trebarvah Farm" ahead, climb the stile in the corner beside a gate and pass through the farmyard. Near a barn follow the signed route across a stile onto an established path through meadowland with Perranuthnoe visible ahead. Head downhill to a stile, shortly after which the path crosses arable land into the village, joining the lane almost opposite the Victoria Inn.

Mounts Bay

Roseland Inn, Philleigh

The Roseland Inn is a 16th century cob-built Cornish gem tucked away on a quiet lane beside the church in the tiny village of Philleigh. The village in the 17th century was on the main road from London to Land's End which crossed the River Fal via what is now the King Harry Ferry two miles away. The inn is a charming place inside and out, the pretty whitewashed exterior has roses climbing around its walls and doors. Inside, the cottage-like atmosphere is maintained with old fashioned seats, a lovely oak settle and sturdy tables dotted around the worn slate floors. Low black beams, half-timbered walls, an old wall clock, attractive bunches of fresh flowers and the warming winter fire enhance the cosy unspoilt charm making it very difficult to leave. Local photographs, gig racing memorabilia and a corner dedicated to rugby trophies and mementoes – both passions of the landlord – adorn the walls. A larger dining room has a huge fireplace and a stable door leading out onto the terrace.

The Roseland is a Devenish pub extremely well run by the new licensee Graham Hill who intends to maintain the standards and reputation created by the previous long serving landlord. Well conditioned Cornish Original and Flowers I.P.A. are the regular real ales plus a guest ale. All are served from the unusual bar area which is set lower than the main rooms.

Excellent, freshly prepared bar food is served daily from 12 noon till 2.15 p.m. and from 6.30 p.m. till 9.15 p.m. The lunchtime menu includes pâté wrapped in bacon, ½ pint of prawns, Hunters ploughmans with cheese, ham, beef and pâté, a range of sandwiches and filled jacket potatoes. This menu is also available in the evenings along with more imaginative home-cooked dishes such as éntrecote au poivre, scampi provençale, chicken breast stuffed with crab and served with a cream and mushroom sauce, seafood platter, vegetarian stroganoff and a choice of two dishes from the specials board. Generous puddings include treacle tart and bread and butter pudding.

Families are welcome and there is no objection to well behaved dogs.

Weekday opening times are from 11.30 p.m. till 3 p.m. and from 6 p.m. till 11 p.m. Telephone: (0872) 580254.

Walk No. 26

Village lies two miles off the A3078 Truro to St. Mawes road, signposted at Ruan High Lanes.

Approx. distance of walk: 6 miles. O.S. Map No. 204 SW 871/394.

Park beside the pub or in the lane.

A fairly long but easy going walk, mostly dry underfoot incorporating farmland paths, quiet country lanes, the scenic coastal path and a fascinating ancient trackway. There are two short stretches of main road.

1. Leave the pub, turn left along the lane passing the churchyard entrance and farm on the left. Take the signed pathway "White Lane" off to the left, soon to cross a stone stile into a field and follow the hedge down into the left hand corner. Turn left onto a lane, pass a few houses and proceed uphill to a chapel taking the waymarked footpath on the right towards "Treworthal & Pendower". Shortly, cross a stone stile in the hedge on to a well defined path along the right hand edge of a field. Keep ahead across two more stone stiles then turn right onto a narrow lane through the hamlet of Treworthal. Beyond the houses turn right down another lane (not signed) and remain on the lane to the main A3078.

2. Turn right and walk along the road for approximately 300 yards before turning left onto a lane towards "Rosevine". At the sharp right hand bend proceed ahead towards "Curgurrell Farm". Enter the farmyard and keep right of the house to join the path down towards the coast. Cross a stile then pass through a wooden gate and bear left towards the coast path sign ahead. Turn right with views across Gerrans Bay to Nare head and round a small headland to a stile and small footbridge. Follow the well defined coast path across three stiles then bear diagonally right uphill to another stile and a fork in the paths beyond. Take the right hand path uphill, pass through a wooden gate then keep right of a large house

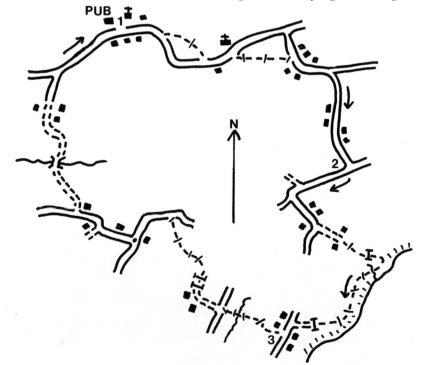

(hotel) and follow the driveway out onto a lane. Turn left and shortly turn right onto a waymarked footpath beside a large fir hedge and pass to the rear of a garden to a stile.

3. Proceed straight across the field ahead, downhill across a brook and stile then uphill to cross a wall stile in the hedge on the right. Bear left across a large field to a stile beside a gate and cross the lane into the driveway of "Pollaughan" (footpath not signed). Keep to the left of the farmhouse and barns to a gate on the right. Follow the right hand hedge, go through another gate then bear diagonally left across the field to a wooden wall stile. Follow the yellow marker arrows half-right across the next field to a wall stile and cross the following three fields via stiles to the main road. Turn left, shortly to turn right onto a quiet lane signed "Lanhoose & King Harry Ferry" and proceed downhill. At Penhaligans Cottage take the waymarked public by-way on the right and follow this fine old trackway downhill across a small brook. Head uphill soon to bear right towards some houses where the by-way becomes metalled. Remain on the lane bearing right at the end onto a lane back into Philleigh and the pub.

A view taken during the walk.

The Rashleigh Arms, Polkerris

The Rashleigh Arms is better known locally as the "Inn on the Beach" for its setting is quite magnificent, tucked down in a tiny cove beside an isolated beach and a restored jetty. The pub is named after the Rashleigh family who once owned the large estate of Menabilly which was more recently the home of Daphne du Maurier. The pub used to be the lifeboat station and the beach shop next door the old lifeboat house until 1924 when it was moved to nearby Fowey. A pub did exist beside the beach on what is now the Rashleigh's car park and was known as the General Elliot but was washed away along with some cottages by a violent storm. Popular with visitors to the pub is the window seat in the main bar, a lovely spot from which to watch the setting sun across St. Austell Bay. The bar has a part carpeted wooden floor, cushioned wall bench seating and chairs. A smaller plusher room with upholstered wall seats and chairs leads up to comfortable restaurant area with superb views.

The pub is a free house very well run by the owners Bernard and Carole Smith. Two real ales, Dartmoor Best Bitter and Burton Ale are on hand pump and the strong local brew St. Austell Hicks Special is served straight from the wood.

A good choice of bar food is available seven days a week with the extensive lunchtime cold buffet a popular event. Also on the menu are a wide range of sandwiches including their special large open sandwiches, ploughmans, soups, fish pie, cottage pie, beef curry and a vegetarian selection such as a lentil shepherds pie and a wholemeal pasta and mushroom bake. Specials are chalked on the blackboard and usually include fresh fish cod fillet, grilled Fowey sea trout and lemon sole. A wide choice of puddings can be chosen from a table in the restaurant. Bar food is available 11 a.m. till 2 p.m. and 6 p.m. till 10 p.m., the restaurant is open Wednesday to Saturday 7 p.m. till 9.30 p.m.

Children are welcome only if eating or if the weather is particularly inclement. Dogs are not allowed.

Weekday opening times are 11 a.m. till 11 p.m. in July and August, at other times 11 a.m. till 2.30 p.m. (flexible) and 6 p.m. till 11 p.m.

Telephone: (072681) 3991.

Village situated off the A3082 between Fowey and Par.

Approx. distance of walk: 3½ miles. O.S. Map No. 204 SX 093/521.

Parking is limited at the pub but there is a large car park up the hill (charge).

An enjoyable gentle walk along the cliff path to Gribben Head and its 84ft. beacon built in 1832 to help vessels navigate safely around the headland and affording open views across St. Austell Bay to Dodman Point and east towards Fowey returning through the Menabilly estate.

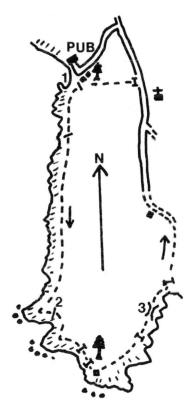

1. From the pub and beach slipway bear left uphill behind the small beach shop then turn right up some steps to follow the way-marked coast path as it zig-zags uphill through woodland. Emerge into an open field, turn right at the fingerpost along the field edge across a stile soon with fine views across to Praa Sands. Shortly, bear right off the field onto the cliff path which undulates to a stile then becomes fairly level in gradient passing through thick vegetation which is alive with many species of finches and migrants in summer.

2. Soon round Little Gribben, cross a wooden stile, turn right onto a track and head towards the red and white beacon on Gribben Head. Pass through a gate onto National Trust land then keep right to another small gate and cross grassland to the beacon which is occasionally open and can be climbed for panoramic all round views. From the beacon follow the wide grassy path downhill through a wooden gate and bear right down to Polridmouth Cove.

3. Cross a small footbridge then shortly leave the coast path, bearing left uphill through a wooden gate. Join a wide trackway, pass to the right of Menabilly Barton farm onto the metalled driveway uphill to a lane. Remain on this quiet lane with the open parkland adjoining Menabilly House to the right, pass Tregaminion chapel then shortly turn left through a metal gate onto a pathway towards woodland. Here rejoin the coast path and outward route downhill through the wood back to the cove and pub.

Key to Symbols

═══ road	---------- track	---------- undefined path
✓ stile	⌣ bridge	⊢—⊣ gate
⊣ ⊢ gap in hedge	⊟ cattle grid	

The Blue Peter, Polperro

Polperro is the most picturesque and photogenic of all the Cornish fishing villages, nestling in a green valley snaking inland from a small harbour guarded by jagged rocks. On the quay at the end of the maze of narrow lanes and alley ways is the Blue Peter, a rustic and unspoilt little fishing pub that is built into the cliffside and overlooks the quaint harbour. Despite being in a very touristy village the pub retains a good local atmosphere, for it is a popular meeting place for the fishermen. The small low beamed bar is lively in the summer as locals vie for space with the influx of holiday-makers, but out of season there is a more relaxed feel to the place. A nautical theme prevails in the cosy dimly-lit bar, fishing nets hang from the ceiling, boat pictures adorn the walls and various mariners bric-a-brac decorate the bar. Furnishings are sturdy and old and include pews, settles and a seat made from an old cask, all of which are never too far from the two open log fires that warm the bar. Piped jazz and blues music generally fills the bar. Upstairs is a room which accommodates children, especially in the summer months. There are two tiny terraces for fine weather drinking.

The pub is a free house owned by Tim Horn. The regular real ales are St. Austell Hicks Special and Tinners Ale and a changing selection of guest beers, such as Exmoor Gold, all of which are dispensed on hand pump.

Good hearty home-made food is on offer here between 12 noon and 3 p.m. and 7 p.m. till 9.30 p.m. and all day during July and August. A blackboard menu displays a good range of dishes such as a home prepared carrot and coriander soup followed by pork in scrumpy, chilli, steak and Guinness pie, freshly cooked pizzas and a selection of fresh fish dishes – sole, plaice or maybe mackerel, caught that morning and brought to the pub from the boat 50 yards away. Vegetarian dishes feature well here – cauliflower and potato bake, lentil and vegetable curry and nut roast in a tomato sauce. Puddings include treacle tart and chocolate fudge cake. Children have their own menu.

Children are welcome in the family room upstairs in the summer and in the bar only in the winter months.

Weekday opening times are from 11 a.m. till 11 p.m.

The village is situated at the end of the A387, west of Looe.

Approx. distance of walk: 4½ miles. O.S. Map No. 201 SX 210/510.

The only place to park in Polperro is at the main car park at Crumplehorn (charge), ten minutes walk from the harbour.

A very scenic and undulating cliff top walk, returning along a peaceful lane. Fairly strenuous in places, but easy going underfoot.

1. From the car park at Crumplehorn follow the lane past the Mill down into Polperro. At the harbour, keep to the west side for the Blue Peter and the quay. Climb the steps behind the pub, waymarked to the cliff and follow the coast path with superb views of this attractive and bustling harbour to the rocky headland and Chapel Cliff (NT). From this popular viewing point take the lower path along the cliff. The path meanders past a few bad-weather shelters before joining the main pathway. Pass through the gorse and scrub covered cliff, the path at this point gently undulating westwards with exceptional coastal views. From a combe on leaving Chapel Cliff, a strength-sapping climb of 150 wooden steps leads you to the top of Raphael Cliff. Drop down into a steep combe, cross a footbridge over a tiny brook and climb the stone steps out of the valley for views across to Pencarrow Head. Descend and climb out of another combe, shortly to head downhill past a stone pillar towards another valley. With a gorse and bracken slope to your right lookout for a stone ladder stile over the fence on the right.

2. Ascend steeply up a grass slope on a narrow well defined path. At the top follow the wire fence on the right inland, gradually climbing uphill towards an old barn visible on the horizon. Keep to the fence, then a wall, pass through a wooden gate, your path (yellow arrow) soon bears left uphill across the pasture to the barn. Pass a fingerpost, then keep right of the barn to a gate. Fine views behind, on a clear day the Lizard Peninsula can be seen. A yellow arrow waymarks the route ahead along a hedged track. Follow this to a country lane noting the views inland to Bodmin Moor and in good weather to Dartmoor.

3. Turn right along this narrow high banked lane. Pass Raphael farm and later Landaviddy Manor Hotel and proceed downhill towards Polperro. Pass a parking area on the left, then just beyond a road sign bear off right onto a metalled lane, beneath a house called Brackens. The lane soon deteriorates into a track affording interesting views down into the valley across Polperro. Keep right of a garage onto a footpath through the edge of woodland. Go down a few steps with metal railings and shortly emerge back onto Chapel Cliff. Join the main footpath, turning left back to the headland viewpoint and the outward route to the pub and harbour.

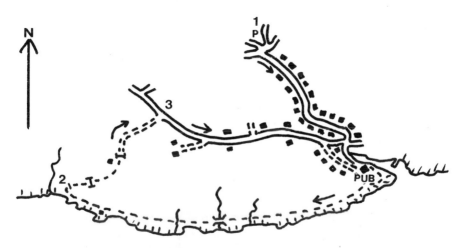

Port Gaverne Hotel – Port Gaverne

This delightful 17th century inn is set in a charming unspoilt cove, just around the corner from the busier and larger fishing harbour of Port Isaac. Although the sea is not visible from the bars, it can be seen if relaxing on the raised terrace outside or from some of the bedrooms by those who are residing at this tranquil haven. A highly polished slate floor leads into the main lounge which has half wood panelled walls, padded wall bench seating, a warming open fire and various watercolours adorn the wall, many of which are for sale. The Wheelhouse or tiny snug bar has a collection of china, old local seafaring photographs, a genuine ship's table, a carved chest and an interesting diorama of the port years ago. On route to the comfortable dining room and the hotel reception is a further seating area with cushioned wall seating and a few local photographs. Everything is spick and span in this relaxing hostelry.

The inn has been in the capable hands of Frederick and Midge Ross for the past 24 years and has become a firm holiday favourite for many regulars. A free house serving St. Austell Hicks Special and Flowers IPA on hand pump.

In summer months and every Sunday throughout the year value-for-money lunchtime bar food is served buffet-style in the dining room. Good snacks include Cornish crab soup, fish pie, cottage pie, steak and kidney pie, various salads – fresh local crab and lobster, ploughmans, sandwiches and there is a separate menu for vegetarians. In the evenings snacks are available in the bar, while the restaurant serves more elaborate fare such as fresh fish, rack of lamb, roast duck and chateaubriand – for two people. Puddings range from crème brulée to summer pudding. Sunday roasts. Food is available daily between 12 noon and 2 pm and from 7 pm till 9.30 pm.

Children are welcome inside, away from the bar.

Weekday opening times are from 11 am till 2.30 pm and 6 pm till 9.30 pm. The inn is closed most of January and February.

Accommodation is available in nineteen double rooms.

Telephone: (0208) 880244.

Port Gaverne lies ½ mile north of Port Isaac, off the B3267.

Approx. distance of walk: 3½ miles. O.S. Map No. 200 SX 003/808.

The inn has a car park up a side lane and there is a small public car park by the cove.

A short but enjoyable walk through the traditional and unspoilt fishing village of Port Isaac, then across peaceful inland valley farmland. Ideal for families, yet some sections can be muddy.

1. Upon leaving the inn walk along the lane to the cove and T-junction. Cross the lane, turn left and shortly join a pavement, follow the road uphill out from the sheltered harbour. Round the headland with fine views north to Tintagel Head and enter the limits of Port Isaac. Bear off right into the car park, join a pitted trackway and pass in front of Castle Rock Hotel. Soon bear right again at the coast path sign onto a tarmac path and walk in front of houses, all the time following the headland round into the magnificent natural harbour of Port Isaac. On reaching a village lane, bear right downhill into the quaint village centre. Pass colourful fishing boats and sheds, bearing left uphill away from the cove.

2. Follow Church Hill, pass the telephone box and take the footpath left, waymarked Trewetha ¾, opposite the house called Jackdaws. This narrow path drops down into a steep-sided valley. Pass through a metal gate, round the edge of sewage works to a wooden gate. A yellow arrow points your way along the valley bottom. Pass in front of a house, along its driveway to a fingerpost directing you left downhill, then along a wire fence inland. At a post with arrows, keep ahead to a stone stile, then along what can be a muddy path through a small woodland. Emerge out onto open valley pasture – good buzzard terrain – and proceed inland, parallel to the stream. Where the valley path begins to bear right lookout for a small footbridge and stone stile on your left. Cross the stream, turn right, pass through a gate and gradually climb out of the valley. Go through a gap in the hedge and bear half-left across the field towards the farmhouse ahead. Beyond a gate, follow the track uphill to the farm and another two gates.

3. Bear right in front of the ancient castellated farmhouse and where the drive veers right, pass through the gate ahead, turn sharp left uphill along the edge of the field to a stone stile. Keep ahead to the right of telegraph pole to another stile in hedge, then head across the field, shortly to follow the line of telegraph poles right across two fields, via gates, to a B-road. Turn left on the road, pass a new house, then cross a stile on the right and proceed ahead along a defined wide track, downhill towards a copse. Pass through the group of trees to another stile in a wire fence, then head downhill into the wooded valley bottom. Pass through the scrub and quite dense wood in the corner of the field, eventually reaching the main valley pathway. Turn left to the stile at the woodland edge and remain on the defined path across two more stiles back into Port Gaverne and the inn.

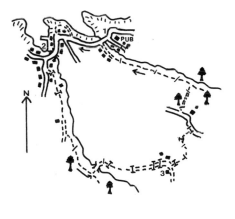

Key to Symbols

══════ road	┄┄┄┄ track	┄┄┄┄ undefined path
/ stile	⌒ bridge	├──┤ gate
─┤ ├─ gap in hedge	▭ cattle grid	

Five Pilchards Inn, Porthallow

Porthallow or "P'raller" as it is locally pronounced was originally a bustling fishing community and until very recently an important area for quarrying roadstone at nearby Porthkerris Point. The hub of this tiny, isolated community is the Five Pilchards, an attractive pub situated on the edge of the beach overlooking Falmouth. The 300 year old building is full of seafaring memorabilia with old ships' lamps, steering wheel, model ships in cases and local prints and photographs of bygone days around Porthallow. A corner of the bar is dedicated to the history of shipwrecks, and a plate recovered from one of these wrecks is encased on the wall. The only bar has rustic feel with pine settles and stools and polished wooden tables. A lobster pot and various gleaming brass pots and pans adorn the ceiling, while a huge woodburner warms the bar on wild winter nights. There is a sheltered courtyard to the side of the pub with bench seating.

David Tripp, born and bred in the village has owned the Five Pilchards for 28 years and has no desire to change the unspoilt and traditional atmosphere of the pub. Being a free house the choice of real ales changes regularly. On my visit well conditioned Greene King Abbot Ale, Cornish Original and Flowers Original were available. There is fine collection of fruit wines and a particularly good Cornish mead from Penzance.

Bar food is served at lunchtimes only, every day except Friday between 12 noon and 2 p.m. The daily changing menu is chalked up on the blackboard and the freshly prepared dishes may include a couple of hearty soups, a range of sandwiches, ploughmans, chicken, gammon and a choice of fresh fish depending on availability. Local crab is used for sandwiches and salads and generally fresh pilchards and mackerel are on offer along with an excellent fish pie. The pub is well known locally for its Sunday roasts.

Children are not allowed in the pub. Dogs are welcome if kept on a lead.

Weekday opening times are from 12 noon till 3 p.m. and 6.45 p.m. till 11 p.m.

Self-catering accommodation is available.

Telephone: (0326) 280256.

Remote Porthallow harbour lies 2 miles from the end of the B3293 in St. Keverne on an unclassified lane.

Approx. distance of walk: 4 miles. O.S. Map No. 204 SW 798/232.

There is a large car park beside the beach opposite the pub (charge) and there is some parking in the lane.

An enjoyable walk along the coast path, around the mouth of the Helford River into the picturesque Gillan Creek returning across farm tracks, along a country lane and down through a peaceful valley back to Porthallow. The going is fairly easy underfoot but the route is undulating.

1. Leave the pub and follow the lane ahead soon to follow the coast path acorn and arrow sign along the top of the beach. Ascend the concrete steps beside some cottages, disregard the path signed to the left remaining on the path around the edge of Porthallow Cove. Cross a stone stile into a field and keep to the right-hand edge, shortly, drop down onto a grassy path which traverses the gently shelving cliff. The cliff here is covered with a mixture of fern, gorse and brambles which provide a good habitat for finches and stonechats. Cross a wall stile into an open field, bear right down a steep hill and follow the field edge around the headland uphill to a wall. Follow the waymarked coast path over the low wall then uphill on the well defined path towards Nare Head.

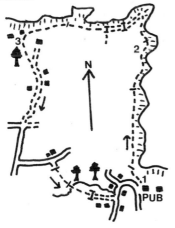

2. Once over the headland the mouth of the Helford River comes into view. Cross a stile and follow the right-hand edge of the field to Nare Point with views across the river mouth and up the coast to Falmouth and St. Mawes. Turn left onto a grassy track following the river's edge inland. Pass through a metal gate then shortly bear right through a swing gate, go across a small footbridge and proceed along a peaceful grassy path from which at low tide oystercatchers can be seen feeding on the rocky foreshore. Cross a wall stile and head sharply uphill soon with views into the sheltered natural harbour of Gillan. Pass a house on the left then drop down three flights of stone steps shortly to emerge beside a small cove on the edge of the village of Gillan.

3. Bear left beside a wooden boathouse following the pathway uphill through mature woodland and bear right onto an unmetalled lane. Remain on this lane through a farmyard where the surface becomes concrete and proceed uphill to a junction of lanes. Go straight ahead onto a narrow, quiet country lane turning first left signed "Porthallow". Head downhill and soon pass Treglossick farm on the left, turning right opposite the yard onto a grassy track to cross a wall stile beside a metal gate. Bear left to join an established pathway beyond a stile then descend down into a valley. Cross the brook at the bottom, remain on the path through the wood then out across open meadows along the valley side. Eventually drop down to some cottages and pass through a kissing gate to follow the path in front of the cottages to a lane. Turn left remaining on the lane round to the beach and the pub.

The Old Pandora Inn, Restronguet Creek

This medieval, quaint old thatched inn is unrivalled in Cornwall for its superb position beside a peaceful creek, complete with patio and pontoon for fine weather. Parts of the building date back to the 13th century when there was a farm on the site and later was known as the "Passage House" when a ferry operated across the creek. It was then called the Ship and finally re-named the "Pandora" in memory of the naval ship sent to Tahiti to capture the mutineers of Captain Bligh's Bounty. The old-world interior has polished black painted flagged floors, low wooden ceilings, wall panelling and rustic wall benches throughout its unspoilt, traditional layout. There is a black painted kitchen range in one bar and a huge log fire in a high hearth in the main bar. The Pandora is very popular in summer with people arriving by boat.

The inn is a St. Austell pub very well run by Roger and Helen Hough. Three real ales are available: Hicks Special, Tinners Ale and Bass.

Bar food is consistently good and served seven days a week. The comprehensive menu includes the popular large sandwiches known as the Pandora Club – chicken, bacon, tomato, lettuce and mayonnaise, Ferryman – cheese, ham, pickled onion and granary bread and Greek-pitta bread stuffed with egg, tuna, mayonnaise. Other dishes range from Restronguet fish pie, Pandora burgers, crab salad, moules marinière, mushroom and watercress soup, seafood hor's-d'oeuvre and chicken and asparagus pie. Puddings may include treacle tart, fruit crumble and lemon meringue pie. Children have their own menu. The low-ceilinged restaurant upstairs serves fresh local fish and is popular for its peaceful river views. Bar food is served between 12 noon and 2 p.m. and 6.30 p.m. to 9.30 p.m., in summer till 2.30 p.m. and 10 p.m. Afternoon teas are served throughout the summer months.

Children are welcome in certain areas of the bar and there is no objection to dogs if they are kept on a lead.

During the summer the pub is open weekdays from 11 a.m. till 11 p.m. and Sunday from 12 noon till 10.30 p.m. although no alcohol is served between 3 p.m. and 7 p.m. Winter times are from 12 noon till 2.30 p.m. and 6.30 p.m. 11 p.m.

Telephone: (0326) 372678.

The creekside hamlet is best reached from the A39 in Penryn signed Mylor Bridge, Flushing, then follow Restronguet Passage signs from Mylor Bridge.

Approx. distance of walk: 5 miles. O.S. Map No. 204 SW 814/372.

The pub has an adequate car park.

A delightful easy walk for the whole family along wooded creekside paths with fine views across the Carrick Roads and Restronguet Creek.

1. Leave the inn and turn right along a gravel lane which passes between numerous creekside cottages affording good views across the creek to Restronguet Point. At Restronguer Weir the path goes along the top of the beach, or use the alternative permitted path at high tide to a lane. Turn left following the waymarked route to "Greatwood" and pass through the gate of "Treweir House". Keep left, soon to join a narrow, sheltered path along the creek edge and emerge onto a gravel lane into the isolated hamlet of Greatwood.

2. Shortly bear right uphill following footpath signed "Mylor Bridge" around the back of Greatwood House with its Scotsbaronial-style tower. On reaching its driveway turn right uphill then turn left onto a footpath downhill through a metal gate into mature oak woodland towards the waterside. From the old quay - Greatwood Quay - there are open views across Mylor Creek to Mylor Churchtown and out across the broad

expanse of Carrick Roads to the Roseland Peninsula. Remain on the well defined pathway which bears right along the creek edge to follow Mylor Creek inland. Continue through a number of fields and gates towards Mylor Bridge. Bear right onto a lane then shortly drop down to the creekside, pass the Post Office into the village centre.

3. Turn right along the main street then turn left into the lane signed "Truro". After fifty yards turn right into Bells Hill and follow the lane uphill. Pass the lane to Restronguet Barton on the right, then take the second track on the right following the orange arrow. Remain on this track which soon descends across three cattle grids down to the river edge with superb views over to Devoran and Penpol Creek. Pass in front of a large white house onto a wooded creekside path which eventually joins an unmetalled lane back to Restronguet Passage and the pub.

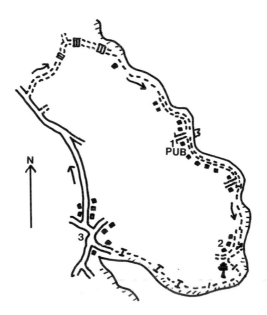

The Old Inn, St. Breward

This low white painted stone cottage claims to be the highest pub in Cornwall at 825ft., set on the edge of Bodmin Moor in one of the most unspoilt areas of the county and in a true Cornish village. Parts of the inn date back over a thousand years when it was a beer house for the builders of the church, which stands just up the lane and dominates the landscape for miles around. A worn carved stone cross to set in the small front lawn and it is said to be of Saxon origin. Beyond the deep entrance porch a warm welcome pervades in the atmospheric bars, the larger than life landlord greets a mixed clientele from locals to farmers and walkers. Slate floors, part exposed stone walls, huge granite fireplace, large old sturdy tables and an assortment of chairs help maintain the rustic charm of this unprententious village pub. Various tools, traps, brasses, a banknote collection and slate paintings for sale decorate the bars. Electronic games and a pool table are sensibly located in a separate room to the rear of the pub.

The pub is a free house and efficiently run by Iain and Ann Cameron. Real ale features well here with a choice of four beers – Ruddles County, Wadworth 6X, Bass and John Smiths Bitter – all dispensed by hand pump. The well stocked bar also has a fine range of malt whiskies.

Hearty snacks are served seven days a week and are popular with locals and walkers. Blackboard specials are all home-cooked and may include a monster moorland grill, steak and kidney pie, carbonnade of beef, smoked seafood platter and for pudding – blackberry and apple crumble and banoffi pie. Good sandwiches and ploughmans, among other snacks are excellent value. A separate menu is available in the evenings in the small restaurant. Food is served from 12 noon till 2 p.m. and 6.30 p.m. till 9.45 p.m. (6 p.m. till 10 p.m. in summer).

Children are welcome in the games room and in the restaurant and well-behaved dogs are allowed in.

Weekday opening times are from 12 noon till 3 p.m. and 6 p.m. till 11 p.m.

Telephone: (0208) 850711.

Village is signposted off the B3226 south of Camelford and off the A30 east of Bodmin. The lanes are narrow.

Approx. distance of walk: 2½ miles. O.S. Map No. 200 SX 098/774.

The inn has a car park.

This walk may be short but it offers superb open views towards the coast from high rough pastures and a peaceful stretch along the River Camel.

1. From the pub turn right along the lane, uphill past the church and The Gables B. & B. Take a waymarked footpath on the left through gorse and scrub with panoramic views ahead towards the coast. Where the grassy path splits bear off right to a wooden gate (white disc) and continue downhill to a granite stile. The path becomes narrow, passing through bramble and bracken following the wall to your right. Soon, on reaching a junction of paths veer diagonally left onto a further narrow path (ill-defined in places) which double backs slightly before descending into the valley. At a wide well established grass path, turn right and head downhill towards a house. The wooded River Camel valley lies ahead – a favourite spot for soaring buzzards. On arriving at a wooden gate turn left onto a wide path which follows the valley side with peaceful views. This delightful bracken-edged path leads you to a wooden gate and an old oak woodland.
2. Enter the wood and gradually head downhill to a T-junction of tracks. Here bear left to a metal gate, beyond which follow an old lane uphill to join another farm track, with a chicken shed to the left. Bear right along this track (extremely muddy after rain) to a gate and a farm. Pass through the gate, bear left along the metalled lane to where it turns sharp left uphill past a house. Keep ahead, through the wooden gate, then to the left of an open fronted barn to another gate. A defined path through pasture leads you through a gap in a hedge, then along the left hand edge of trees. Shortly, veer left on a well defined trackway through the beech and hazel woodland to a wall stile. Cross over, then pass through a wooden gate into an enclosure of a rare breeds animal sanctuary. Follow the fence ahead – deer were in the enclosure beyond – pass through a gate and follow the arrowed path through the sanctuary with ponds away to your right and enclosures to the left. Cross a stone stile and footbridge and shortly join a lane.
3. Turn left and follow the lane up a steep hill, passing a waterfall to your left. At a T

junction next to stone house bear left towards an old corrugated workshop, cross the stream and turn right onto a footpath along the edge of the stream, then into woodland. Head uphill parallel to the stream, cross a small tributary and emerge out onto an open bracken area. Superb views across the Camel valley. Keep on the boulder strewn path, bearing left uphill. Soon bear right across a stone stile, pass between two bungalows to a lane. Turn left at footpath sign to Tucking Mill and follow pitted lane past houses and North Cornwall Aviaries. Cross a cattle grid, then just before a cottage bear right up a grassy bank into an open pasture. Turn half-right to a stone wall stile and turn left between the wall and conifer trees to another stile. Keep left handed along the edge of a school playing field to a stile, then proceed ahead along a walled footpath to a wooden gate. Continue ahead towards the church and the pub.

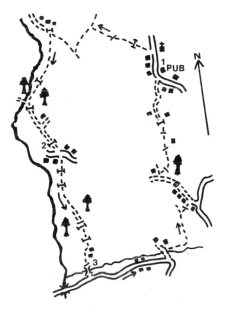

The Rising Sun, St. Mawes

The Rising Sun is a lively little hotel set in an enviable position just across the lane from the sea wall, overlooking the quaint anchorage of St. Mawes harbour and its 19th century quay. The inn is certainly the heart of village life, busy with visitors in the height of the season. The small, simply furnished public bar is carpeted with cushioned wall seats, especially the much-coveted window seat with harbour views. An open fire warms this tiny bar on stormy winter nights and local photographs of bygone St. Mawes decorate the walls. The locals bar is contrasted with the modern, south-facing conservatory which leads out onto the front terrace. This airy bar has cushioned cane chairs, dark plush upholstered bench seats, white boarding, lots of brass, plants and dried flowers as well as harbour views.

The inn is owned by the St. Austell Brewery and serves two of their real ales, Hicks Special and Bosun's Cornish Bitter on hand pump.

An excellent range of home-cooked food is available in the bars, the main menu being supplemented by a typed list of daily specials. Dishes may include brocolli and fennel soup, moules, lamb curry, seafood tagliatelle, medallions of pork, stuffed peppers, baked stuffed fish, various jacket potatoes and steaks. Snacks include ploughmans and a good range of sandwiches. For pudding choose from sherry trifle, mixed berry cheesecake and lemon and almond tart. In summer months non-residents can enjoy breakfast here between 8.30 a.m. and 9.30 a.m., lunch from 12 noon till 2.30 p.m., afternoon tea between 3 p.m. and 5 p.m. and evening meals from 6 p.m. till 9.30 p.m. There is a also a barbeque most evenings from 9.45 p.m. till 10.45 p.m. The popular restaurant serves more ambitious meals and is open Monday to Saturday evenings from 7.30 p.m. till 9.30 p.m., and for Sunday lunch. Children have their own menu.

Children are allowed in the conservatory bar and restaurant if eating. Dogs are welcome in the public bar.

Weekday opening times are from 11 a.m. till 2.30 p.m. and from 6 p.m. till 11 p.m. In summer from 8.20 p.m. till 11 p.m.

The inn has twelve letting bedrooms.

Telephone: (0326) 270233.

Village lies at the end of the Roseland Peninsula on the A3078, overlooking Falmouth.

Approx. distance of walk: 5½ miles. O.S. Map No. 204 SW 848/331.

There is a large public car park beside the inn (charge).

An enjoyable fairly level and easy going walk along the edge of the Fal estuary and the peaceful Percuil Creek. The walk explores the delightful churchyard at St. Just in Roseland and offers superb open views.

1. Turn left from the pub along the road, soon to join the pavement and head away from the harbour. Bear round to the left through residential area, then at Freshwater Lane turn sharp right downhill by the 30mph sign towards the creek. At the quay, turn left onto footpath signed "Percuil Creek", which runs between hedges at the bottom of gardens. Turn right onto a track, then left across a slipway to join a narrow path along the river's edge. Fine river views across to St. Anthony.

2. Keep to this peaceful and scenic path to a stile beside a bungalow. Go over and keep to the right hand edge of the field before bearing left uphill with the yellow arrow when parallel to a house on your right. Pass into scrubland, then where the path forks, keep ahead through gorse, shortly to bear left through a gateway. Proceed ahead on a visible grass track gently uphill, with good views, to a stile beside a metal gate. Cross over and follow the right hand hedge to two gates, then bear left into a cul-de-sac. Walk through the small estate, turning left at junction for the main road.

3. Turn right along the main road – taking care – following a pavement, then a narrow grassy verge for ½ mile to a water tower beyond St. Mawes garage. At the entrance to a track on your left across a stile into National Trust land – Tregear Vean, the footpath signed to "St. Just". Keep to the right hand edge, parallel to the road across a series of stiles and fields, with panoramic views across the Fal estuary, Falmouth and beyond over rolling countryside. Follow the waymarked path left along a track, across a stile and proceed downhill to another stile. Bear left onto a driveway beside a house and drop down to a lane and the lych-gate to St. Just in Roseland.

4. Enter the magnificient churchyard, which lies beside a tranquil creek, and walk through the "sub-tropical" terraced grounds, resplendent with palms, shrubs, flowers and ponds and follow the pathway left along the creekside to a wooden swing-gate. The footpath soon drops onto the shingle. Keep left in front of Pascoes Boatyard onto a metalled lane. Shortly bear right "St. Mawes 2m" into a driveway passing Bar Pont House. Keep left around the bungalow ahead, cross a stone stile onto an established path across open meadowland, with views to Falmouth. The path is well defined and level from here, crossing the low cliff via stiles to St. Mawes. On nearing the village pass through a gate onto a metalled lane to St. Mawes Castle. Turn right downhill into the village, bearing left around the harbour back to the pub.

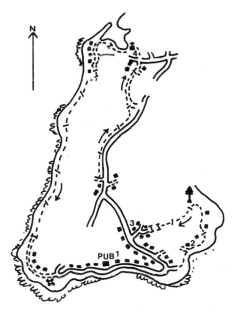

The Falcon Inn, St. Mawgan

St. Mawgan lies surrounded by woodland in the deep, sheltered Vale of Lanherne and consists of charming cottages, a turret-towered church, a 13th century manor house and the delightful wisteria-clad Falcon Inn. The 16th century stone inn was known as the Gardeners Arms until the mid 19th century, when an eminent local man decided to change the name to the Falcon Inn after the crest of the long established Willyams family, who have owned the large estate of Carnanton since 1685. The large main bar is carpeted and furnished with upholstered wall benches and a mix of pine farmhouse tables and chairs. Trellis pattern wallpaper brightens up the walls beneath the pine dado rail and tasteful wildlife and hunting prints decorate the cream coloured walls. A large open fire warms this bar. The main dining area has a flagged stone floor covered with Oriental rugs, a pine dresser and French windows leading out into the cobbled courtyard. The garden has won many awards for its floral displays. There is an attractive sheltered terrace area close to the wisteria cloaked walls and a rose covered arch leads to large terraced gardens with benches. The pub can get very busy in the height of the season. The inn is a St. Austell pub extremely well run by licensees Andrew and Helen Banks. Well kept Hicks Special and Tinners Ale are served by hand pump.

A comprehensive bar menu is supplemented with popular daily specials which are chalked up on a blackboard. At lunchtimes there is a choice of salads, soups, sandwiches, ploughmans and hot dishes such as home-made lasagne and steak and kidney pie. Evening fare includes spicy curry, steaks, seafood crèpes, leek and ham mornay, crab soup, chicken Kiev and mushroom and nut fettucini. Puddings range from cheesecake and apple pie to pavlova. Sunday lunches are popular throughout the year. Bar food is served from 11.30 a.m. till 2 p.m. and from 7 p.m. till 9.30 p.m.

Children are welcome in the dining area and there is no objection to dogs.
Weekday opening times are from 11 a.m. till 3 p.m. and from 6 p.m. till 11 p.m.
The inn has two letting bedrooms.
Telephone: (0637) 860225.

Village is signposted off the A3059 5 miles north of Newquay.

Approx. distance to walk: 6¾ miles. O.S. Map No. 200 SW 872/659.

There is a large car park behind the Post Office and Stores.

Although long this is a delightful easy going walk through the wooded Lanherne valley following the tiny Menalhyl river into the historic town of St. Columb Major, once considered as the site for Cornwall's cathedral. Return across farmland, along a country lane and back along the river bank.

1. Leave the inn and turn right alongside St. Mawgan Post Office towards the car park. Bear right beside "Riverside Cottage" to a wooden gate and turn left along a path signed "Lawtrey's Mill and St. Columb". Keep to this peaceful path through mature mixed woodland with the River Menalhyl to your left. On nearing Lawtrey's Mill ignore the pathway leading down to a footbridge, keep ahead behind the old mill on what is now a well defined trackway. Shortly, the track gradually bears round to the right, uphill to another track. Turn left, then left again signed "St. Columb" downhill across a brook to a stile beside a gate on the left. Cross the stile and keep to the right hand edge of the field with superb valley views to another stile and join an old cobbled lane.

2. Follow the lane, descend to cross a stile and a brook and join a narrow metalled lane, remaining on this into the village of St. Columb. On reaching the main street turn left and proceed downhill, forking off left at the telephone box down to the bridge over the river. At the post box in the wall across the bridge turn left along a track in front of some cottages to a stile beside a metal gate. Bear right uphill at a brick building to a stile in the hedge on the left. Cross the brook, bear right across the field to a wall stile then proceed straight across the field to

a wall stile then maintain course across the next field to a stile between gorse bushes. Follow the defined path to another wall stile and footbridge over a brook, then keep to the right hand edge of the field and climb a stile hidden in the hedge beside a wide trackway entrance into the field. Follow the directional arrow left along the field edge looking carefully for a wall stile on the left.

3. Climb the stile, proceed ahead across the farmhouse drive and pass through two wooden gates to the right of a barn. Keep to the left hand edge across the next two fields before passing through the first metal gate in the corner of the field. Turn right, follow the hedge to an overgrown wall stile in the corner, then keep to the right-hand edge of the field downhill to the farmhouse ahead. Proceed through the farmyard, in front of the house and bear right onto the concrete drive uphill to a lane. Turn left and follow the lane to a telephone box, turning left again into the hamlet of Higher Tolcarne. Follow the footpath signed "Lawtrey's Mill and St. Mawgan", then keep left to join a pathway beside "Lanherne Gate" and proceed downhill on an old trackway to a stile beside a gate. Cross this and the footbridge over the river and bear right shortly to join the main Lanherne valley path back to St. Mawgan and the pub.

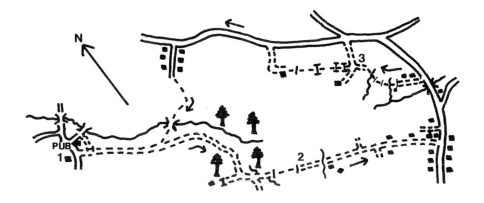

Old Success Inn, Sennen Cove

The location of this old 17th century fisherman's inn is quite superb, in the beautiful Sennen Cove with magnificient sea views across Whitesand Bay to Cape Cornwall. Back in 1850 Sennen was a busy fishing port with 84 fishermen, today only a handful of men earn their living from the sea with the village now prospering on tourism. Whitesand Bay is the perfect family beach, ideal for swimming and surfing. The Old Success is just across the lane from the beach and can get busy in the height of the season. The large whitewashed building has bench seating beside a low stone wall with good sea views. The majority of the inn is given over for accommodation and residents use but the modern and airey "Charlies Bar" is welcoming and offering sea views. The carpeted open plan bar is furnished with modern tables and chairs and local seafaring photographs from bygone days adorn the walls.

The inn is a free house with well kept Bass the only real ale available on draught.

Bar food is served seven days a week from 12 noon till 2.30 p.m. and 7 p.m. till 9.30 p.m. The routine bar menu offers a choice of beef curry, steak and kidney pie, seafood platter, various omelettes, a range of sandwiches plus usually a couple of specials written on the blackboard in the bar and may include excellent fresh fish and on my visit pork satay. Vegetarian dishes are also available as well as a children's menu.

Weekday opening times are from 11 a.m. till 2.30 p.m. and 6.30 p.m. till 11 p.m.

Familes are very welcome.

Telephone: (0736) 871232.

Sennen Cove lies just off the A30 1 mile north of Land's End.

Approx. distance of walk: 4½ miles. O.S. Map No. 203 SW 353/263.

The inn has limited parking but there are two large car parks nearby (charge).

A gently undulating cliff walk around Land's End affording some of the best cliff scenery in Cornwall with a variety of rock formations, perched boulders and pinnacled ridges as well as fine headlands and coves. There is one steep ascent on leaving the coast path.

1. From the inn turn left along the seafront passing the Lifeboat Station and the Round House following the coast path signs uphill towards the castellated lookout for stunning views across Whitesand Bay and ahead to Land's End. Remain on this established stretch of path (in places severely eroded) with superb cliff scenery towards the Land's End complex. Bear right downhill to the First and Last House and join the main path across a wooden suspension bridge for views of Kittiwakes, Fulmars, Shags and Seals.

2. Pass in front of the hotel onto a wide path and shortly bear right onto a narrow path downhill to cross a small footbridge, cross a track following the path to the rear of some animal enclosures. Soon leave this rare breeds unit and craft workshop area behind as the coast path crosses open heathland with fine cliff views. After ½ mile descend into Nanjizal or Mill Bay but do not go down to the beach, turn left up a narrow steep path through heather and gorse away from the sea.

3. The path follows the top of a valley inland. Bear left across a stone stile, head towards Sennen church tower to the far corner of the field and cut the corner of the next field then keep to the wall along the left hand edge to the stone stile. Cross this onto a metalled lane, shortly cross another lane and enter Trevilley farmyard. Cross the steps ahead keep to the right hand edge of a field to a stile then soon pass in front of a cottage to a road. Turn left, shortly cross the A30 onto a waymarked track, go over a stile on the right into lush meadowland where the path is signed "Sennen Cove". Pass through two gates, head towards the white coastguard buildings and cross two stiles keeping close to the wall to a swing gate. Turn left onto a metalled driveway, shortly bear right along a lane at the top of Sennnen Cove for ¼ mile before turning left onto a path signed to the cove downhill to the seafront. Turn right back to the inn.

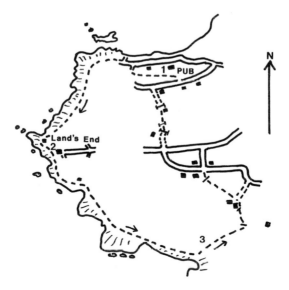

The Port William, Trebarwith Strand

This whitewashed building enjoys a superb position on the cliff-edge, overlooking the inlet and magnificent stretch of sand known as Trebarwith Strand. On warm sunny summer days picnic benches line the edge affording glorious views and are popular with beach sunbathers seeking refreshment. By contrast, on wild stormy winter days it is exhilarating watching the waves crashing on the beach below from the picture windows in the warm and welcoming bar. Open plan in layout the bar has exposed walls, cushioned pew benches and stools for seating, a roaring open fire, while fishing nets and shells adorn the walls and ceiling. Away from the bar area and dining section is a childrens room complete with games.

This busy free house is efficiently run by owners Peter and Gillian Hale. Five real ales are dispensed on hand pump, the regular beers are St. Austell Hicks Special and Tinners Ale and John Smiths Bitter with Mitchells Best and ESB available as guest ales on my visit. Scrumpy Jack Cider is also served.

A comprehensive menu is supplemented by a range of daily blackboard specials, for example – steak and kidney pie, beef curry and fishermans pie. The main menu features hearty snacks such as jumbo rolls, pasties, Port William salad platters and the usual breaded fish hot dishes. More substantial meals can be ordered both lunchtime and evenings, such as lamb steak, fillet of chicken supreme, beef bourguignonne, salmon steak, lasagne, vegetable moussaka and a choice of steaks. Children have their own menu. Food is served between 12 noon and 2 p.m. (2.30 p.m. Sunday) and from 6 p.m. to 9.30 p.m. (from 7 p.m. on Sundays).

Weekday opening times in the winter are from 12 noon till 3 p.m. and 5.30 p.m. till 11 p.m. From Easter till October the pub is open all day from 11 a.m. till 11 p.m.

Children are welcome in the children's room and well-behaved dogs are allowed in the bar.

Telephone: (0840) 770230.

The coastal hamlet of Trebarwith Strand lies 3 miles south of Tintagel, off B3263.

Approx. distance of walk: 3¾ miles. O.S. Map No. 200 SX 050/864.

The pub has its own car park but there is also a car park near the beach.

This invigorating ramble explores Tintagel, its Old Post Office (NT) and the legendary King Arthur's Castle, returning across spectacular cliffs with the still-visible relics of slate quarrying and fine open views.

1. From the pub walk down into the village turning left at the lane towards the beach. Follow the coast path sign right beside the public toilets and begin climbing up onto Treknow Cliff. On reaching a fork in the path bear right inland, along a grassy path, uphill towards a pink-wahsed house. Soon join a wide track and pass between two large houses to a tarmac lane, which soon becomes pitted along the edge of Treknow village. On merging with a lane at Trenowan Hotel bear left with the lane, which affords good sea views. Turn left onto the B3263, following the footway for a short distance to a sharp right hand bend. Keep ahead along a tiny lane, passing a few houses, to a green fingerpost, waymarked Trebarwith, and a junction of paths.

2. Turn right down a stony drive towards a pink house and keep left to a green gate and stile. Cross over and proceed ahead across the field to another stile in the fence. Follow a well-defined path along the left hand hedge towards Tintagel ahead. Beyond the next stile, keep left, passing to the right of a paddock and stable to a stile and wooden gate. Go over onto a waymarked track and shortly turn right down a lane, signed to the village. Pass the Chapel of Fontebrault and climb up into Tintagel. At the T-junction turn right for the Old Post Office and village centre. The main route heads left. Turn left along a slate track beyond Woottons Hotel, following the arrowed route to Tintagel Castle downhill. Cross a small footbridge over a stream on your left. To visit the 12th-13th century remains of King Arthur's Castle remain on the track.

3. Over the stream follow a narrow slatey footpath uphill, pass to the left of a gate and shortly curve left onto the main coast path towards Tintagel Church (worth a visit). Good views of the Castle and Tintagel Head. From the church cross Glebe Cliff (NT) parking area onto a footpath, ignoring tracks either side. Shortly, merge left with a track and where this bears left keep right down towards the magnificently sited Youth Hostel, stuning sea views. Keep right along the cliff-edge to join a narrow path which climbs around Penhallic Point – once the site of a wharf where slate was loaded onto vessels by means of a wooden crane. This narrow path soon rejoins the main coast path with superb views down the coast and across to Gull Rock, opposite Trebarwith Strand. Cross a stone stile onto Bagalow Cliff (NT), pass Hole Beach, then the impressive 80ft. Pinnacle in the once active Lanterdan Quarry onto Treknow Cliff (NT). The path in places passes close to the cliff edge, so take care. The coast path soon begins to descend, rejoining outward route back to Trebarwith Strand and the pub.

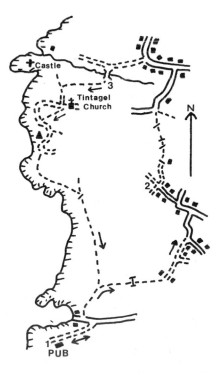

The Logan Rock, Treen

This characterful 400 year old inn is named after a 65 ton rock that teeters precariously on the cliff edge close to the village. In 1824 a Naval Lieutenant levered it out of its position and through the local inhabitants raising such a fuss was forced by the Admiralty to replace it to its original position at a cost to himself of £130. A bill of costs is displayed in the bar and the double-sided pub sign depicts the event, one side showing the rock in place the other showing it dislodged. Rustic charm and character prevails in the thick stone-walled, low ceilinged main bar with its high-backed settles, cushioned wall seats and in winter a warming log fire. Local prints and photographs including a set of prints relating to the Logan Rock replacement adorn the stone walls. There is a smaller well furnished "snug" bar and across the stone passageway the food and family bar. The stone courtyard in front of the pub is resplendent with colourful window boxes and there are tubs on the sheltered rear patio.

The inn is a St. Austell pub enthusiastically run by Peter and Anita George serving two well-conditioned real ales on hand pump, Hicks Special Draught and Tinners Ale.

There is a good choice of bar food, a standard menu is supplemented with hearty daily specials and is served throughout the day between June and September, at other times 12 noon till 2.30 p.m. and 6 p.m. till 9 p.m. (from 7 p.m. in winter). A range of starters include garlic mushrooms, home-made soup, pâté and fish dippers served with tartare sauce. Main dishes include the Logan Rock Seafarer - a fish and cheese crumble, Minack Melody - lentils, tomato, and nuts topped with cheese and Longships Bake - macaroni, fish, celery and vegetables topped with breadcrumbs. Also available are lasagne, a range of steaks, salads, ploughmans, jacket potatoes with various fillings, basket meals and an excellent choice of good sandwiches. Puddings include apple cake, fruit pie, crumbles and ice creams.

Children are welcome in the family room only and a children's menu is available. Dogs are permitted but must be kept under control.

Weekday opening times are from 11 a.m. till 11 p.m.

Telephone: (0736) 810495.

The hamlet of Treen is situated just off the B3315, 3 miles from Lands End.

Approx. distance of walk: 3 miles. O.S. Map No. 203 393/231.

The pub has a small car park but there is a public car park round the corner near the Post Office (charge).

A scenic walk around rugged coastline, dramatic headlands contrasting with sheltered sandy coves followed by a quiet level return route across farmland. There is one steep climb up to the Minack Theatre, an incredible 700 seat amphitheatre hewn into the cliffside 700 metres above the sea and offering audiences a spectacular natural backdrop of sea, sand and cliff scenery. Plays are staged during the summer months in the evenings and the theatre is open to viewing during the day.

1. Leave the pub and turn right shortly to bear left to the Post Office. Bear right onto a track and almost immediately turn left signed "Logan Rock" up a few stone steps to bear left onto a wide farm track. In thirty yards follow the well established and way-marked path on the right across four fields and stone stiles to the coastal footpath. To view the Logan Rock go across onto the headland (NT).

2. Turn right onto the coast path along Treen Cliff (NT), fine views back across crenallated cliffs to the Logan Rock and ahead to the white sands of Porthcurno beach with the Minack Theatre above. At a junction of paths carry straight on, across a stone stile beside a gate and head towards the cable marker on the cliff edge, the path now descends sharply (care to be taken!) down towards the magnificient beach.

3. Cross the main beach path onto a narrow path which gradually ascends the cliff above the beach, pass the sign warning you of the steep climb ahead and begin climbing the stepped route up to the Minack Theatre. Cross the car park go through a small gate back onto the coast path gradually ascending to the next headland. Descend down to the isolated beach at Porthchapel, pass St. Levans Holy Well (water still used for baptisms) then leave the coast path to follow a narrow path inland along a small combe. Bear right across a brook, through a gate shortly to cross a lane into St. Levans churchyard.

4. Leave the churchyard in the far right hand corner by a classic example of an old coffin stile, cross two fields on a well defined path towards the farm ahead. Go through a metal kissing gate, bear left across a park-

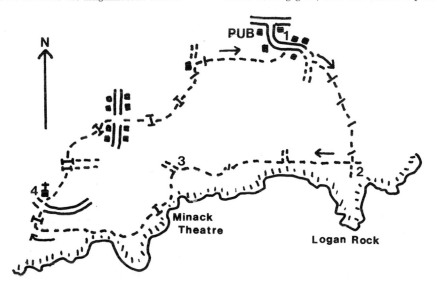

ing area through another swing gate, keep right soon to join a lane and proceed downhill through a gate into Porthcurno village. Cross the lane onto "Cable and Wireless" property, keep to the right of some garages and soon bear off left uphill onto a footpath. Go through a gate following the path towards communication masts ahead and shortly pass close to the post holding the vertical wire up to a gateway.

5. Cross the next two fields via gates, in the third field bear diagonally right to cross a stile to enter the farmyard of Trendrennan Farm and keep right shortly to cross a wall stile on the right opposite the main farmhouse. Follow the left-hand edge of the field, cross a stile in the far corner onto a well established footpath across five fields via stone stiles with good rural inland views. Eventually join a track which bears left onto the lane in Treen, keep left downhill to the pub.

A Sandy Cove on the Walk from Treen

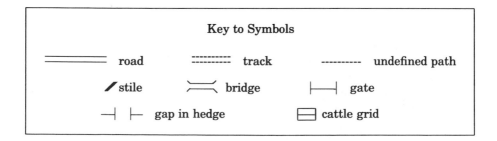

Key to Symbols

road   track   undefined path

stile   bridge   gate

gap in hedge   cattle grid

The Eliot Arms, Tregadillett

Also known as the Square and Compass, this fine 14th century creeper-clad inn has now thankfully been by-passed by the new A30. Inside, a series of five cosy, softly-lit and atmospheric rooms house an amazing collection of memorabilia – its like being in the old curiosity shop as there is so much of interest to catch the eye. Every nook and cranny is filled with an array of horsebrasses, old prints, postcards and photographs, copper ornaments, books, china plates and a superb collection of 66 clocks, including seven grandfather clocks. There is a real assortment of individual furniture, much of it antique, including huge settles, Victorian dining chairs, chaise longues and sturdy wooden tables, topped with fresh flowers. There are open fires and slate floors strewn with rugs and a half wood panelled games room with table skittles and bar billiards. Across the lane is a small sheltered garden and play area for the children.

The inn is a free house, enthusiastically run by the owner John Cook who has gradually created the treasure trove that fills the bars. The well stocked bar features a good wine list and three real ales, namely Flowers Original, Marstons Pedigree and Boddingtons Bitter, all served on hand pump.

Food is a major attraction here and it is available seven days a week from 12 noon till 2 p.m. and 7 p.m. till 9.30 p.m. A printed menu is supplemented by a range of blackboard specials that change twice daily. Generous helpings can be expected with such dishes as beef and vegetable soup, lamb and apricot pie, pork and kidney pie, cottage pie, fresh halibut in a cream and prawn sauces, home-made curries, Greek-style pork kebab, mixed grill and an interesting selection of vegetarian dishes. Puddings are displayed in a cold cabinet and may include fresh fruit salad, pavlova and trifles.

Children are welcome in the eating area and in the front two rooms, as are dogs. The inn has two letting bedrooms.

Weekday opening times are from 11 a.m. till 2.30 p.m. and 6 p.m. till 11 p.m. Telephone: (0566) 772051.

Walk No. 38

Village is signposted off the A30 at the western end of the Launceston by-pass.

Approx. distance of walk: 3½ miles. O.S. Map No. 201 SX 298/838.

The inn has a car park.

An enjoyable short ramble across field paths, tracks and along a quiet lane beside the River Kensey. Some of the farm tracks can be muddy after rain. A good family walk.

1. On leaving the pub turn right along the narrow lane into the main part of the village. At the T-junction bear right to the Methodist Chapel. Just before the chapel turn right by the telephone box onto a track, shortly passing behind some houses. At the end cross a stile flanking a metal gate, then follow the right hand edge of the field to another metal gate where a yellow arrow waymarks the route left along the left hand edge of a field. Good views of rolling countryside and Bodmin Moor. Climb a stile in the field corner and follow the narrow path between a fence and hedgerow to a metal gate. Keep ahead along a wide trackway, pass through another gate, then just at the metalled lane take the signed footpath on your left, through two gates. Keep to the right hand hedge, downhill to a stile beside a gate. Bear left along the hedge down to a wooden gate, then keep to the edge of woodland and shortly bear half-right downhill to a stile on the woodland edge. The arrowed path now descends through the woodland beside a wire fence into the valley. Pass through a gate, out of the wood and bear diagonally left towards the house ahead. Go through a gate and turn left along a quiet lane along the Kensey valley.
2. Remain on this peaceful lane, parallel to the river. On reaching a farmhouse called Tanker's Lake, turn left at a waymarker and pass through two gates into the farmyard. Bear left up a concrete path to a gate, then keep to the muddy track uphill to another gate. The arrowed track soon curves left around the edge of woodland to a gate. Keep ahead beside the wood – which hides an old hill fort – then at the field boundary climb the gate in the hedge on your right. Follow the left hand edge of the field, pass through a gate, then keep left round the hedge before bearing diagonally right to a gate in the right hand corner of the field. Beyond the gate join a hedged trackway towards Kestles Farm (can be muddy). Bear left with the track into the farm complex, then at a crossroads of tracks turn left and pass in front of a bungalow. Where the track bears right, keep ahead with the fingerpost through a metal gate and head across the pasture to a stile in the hedgerow. Bear half-left across the next field to another stile visible in the bank, then bear diagonally left on a defined path to a gate on the edge of woodland. Proceed ahead down through the beech trees, over a small stream, then head uphill with the yellow arrow. Shortly, bear left onto an unmetalled lane back to the Methodist Chapel. Keep right on reaching the lane and retrace steps back to the pub.

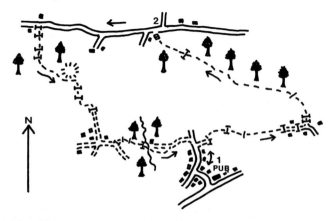

New Inn, Veryan

The tranquil village of Veryan lies in a lush wooded hollow and is best known for its circular 19th century round houses, each topped with a conical thatched roof and a cross. Their shape stems from an old tradition that the devil likes to hide and lie in wait in corners. In 1855 Veryan boasted four pubs, today the New Inn, built in the early 1800's as two cottages, is the only one left. Inside the whitewashed stone exterior is a single carpeted bar that is delightfully simple and unspoilt. Stone fireplaces, each with an old wall oven, warm either end of the long room while padded wall bench seating, captains chairs and low stools surround both square and round pub tables. Brasses and tankards adorn the bar and old photographs adorn the walls. The rustic charm of this village local is enhanced by the absence of piped music and electronic games.

The pub is owned by the St. Austell brewery and excellent Tinners Ale and Bosun's Ale are served straight from the cask.

Hearty homely cooking is the order of the day at the New Inn. The blackboard menu features such favourites as steak and kidney pie, liver and bacon, gammon steak and ploughmans. Other dishes may include cod fillet and chips, plaice stuffed with prawns, beef madras curry, curried chiken and vegetarian dishes like spicy vegetable chilli and vegetable strogannof. The puddings range from hot apple pie to chocolate nut sundae. Bar food is served from 12 noon till 1.45 pm. and 7 p.m. till 9 p.m.

Children are welcome inside if they are eating and there is no objection to dogs being in the bar.

Weekday opening times are from 11.30 a.m. till 3 p.m. and 6.30 p.m. till 11 p.m.

The inn has three letting rooms.

Telephone: (0872) 501362.

Walk No. 39

Veryan is signposted off the A3078 Truro to St. Mawes road.

Approx. distance of walk: 4½ miles. O.S. Map No. 204 SW 916/395.

Parking is limited but it is possible to park on the lane outside the inn.

Enjoyable and scenic coastal ramble exploring Nare Head as well as walking on inland farmland paths from the attractive village of Veryan. A few coast path climbs, otherwise fairly easy going.

1. From the inn turn left to the main village road, then turn right downhill to take the waymarked path opposite the primary school signed to Portloe via Trewartha. Pass to the right of the pond, go through a wooden swing gate and follow the right hand edge of a playing field to the corner. Walk parallel to a small stream to a stile. Proceed ahead with the yellow arrows uphill, keeping to the left of a slate memorial stone and head for the corner of the field. Pass through a metal gate and the small copse beyond to a stone stile. Keep ahead (yellow arrow) across pasture towards an old chapel and a gate. Go through the gate onto a fine hedged green lane, pass to the right of the chapel to a lane. Turn left, then immediately right onto a marked route along a dead-end track. Shortly, turn right in front of Corner Cottage and follow track between cottages to a metal gate. Climb the stone steps over the wall, follow the left hand edge of the field past a stone barn and cross the corner of a field to another wall stile. Bear half-left towards a house, crossing the stile in the wall just before it. Bear right along the wall, through a gate, beside a house and onto a lane after a further gate. You are now in the hamlet of Camels.
2. Proceed ahead along the lane to a sharp left hand bend. Go straight on through a white gateway – Parc Broom (NT), the house featured in the TV series Camomile Lawn – for access to the coastal footpath. Follow the path to the right of the house, join the coast path and head downhill with superb coastal views. The bracken-edged path leads down to a footbridge over a small stream and climb up to a stile, remaining on the coast path. Ascent is quite steep in places, but there are good views along the cliffs to Dodman Point. At the top of the cliff cross a stone wall stile and follow the path close to the cliff edge to the left of a fence, with views out to Gull Rock – used in the 1950's film of Treasure Island and a breeding ground for many seabirds, especially Kittiwakes. Cross a stile and round Kiberick Cove to another stile. Follow the path around the head of the valley (signs), then proceed to Nare Head.

3. With magnificent views, cross the grassy headland towards a gorse outcrop on the tip and bear right to join the narrow coast path downhill into Gerrans Bay. Cross a stile and drop down into the steep-sided Mallet's Cove. Pass the ruin of an old fishermans cottage, then just before a footbridge turn right inland. Cross a stile and proceed up valley through a small copse to a stile. Turn left, follow the edge of the field to a stile located to the right of a gate and enter the car park for Nare Head. Turn left along the lane. Pass a farmhouse, then lookout for the waymarked path across a wall stile on the left. Keep half-left to another wall stile (yellow arrow) and proceed across a further pasture to a stile. Turn right along the field edge to a stile in the far right hand corner and drop down onto a lane.
4. Turn left, pass the entrance to Tregamenna farm and take the arrowed path right over a stile. Head straight across the field looking out for a double stile in the hedge. Turn left with the arrow along a track downhill towards Veryan. Follow the field edge round to a wall stile, then with the wire fence to your right head towards a metal gate. Go through the gate and shortly turn right along a lane, passing between two of the round houses back into Veryan and the pub.

The Tinners Arms, Zennor

The tiny village of Zennor shelters in a hollow just north of the road and is an intriguing place. There is a charming Folk Museum in a cottage containing a traditional Cornish kitchen and a collection of domestic and mining implements. In the 12th century church there is a bench-end carved in the form of a mermaid, the subject of a local legend. Beside the church stands the 14th century Tinners Arms built to accommodate the masons who were extending the church and it was here that D. H. Lawrence drank when he lived in a cottage nearby during the First World War, writing "Woman in Love". Both he and his wife were driven out of the village, suspected of being German spies. The main bar of this slate-roofed, grey stone building has a timeless air about it, remaining unchanged for years. Low ceilings, black beams, wall benches and pews and scrubbed pine tables create the simple, rustic atmosphere that prevails. Two open fires warm the bar in winter and four large prints of old English scenes brighten up the walls. Two other simply furnished rooms are used when busy and are ideal family rooms. There is seating in the ancient courtyard in front of the pub or on the patio to the side of the pub.

David Care has been in charge of this welcoming free house for over 18 years and draws the fruity and hoppy St. Austell Hicks Special from the wood using a quite unusual hand pump.

The short daily changing menu is chalked up on a blackboard which stands on the bar and may include a hearty ploughmans, chicken, ham and mushroom pie, broccoli and cheese bake, stilton and leek bake with apple pie and cream for dessert. Most of the dishes are home-made and served from 12 noon till 3 p.m. and 6 p.m. till 9.30 p.m. although these times are flexible.

Children are welcome in the two rooms away from the bar and there is no objection to dogs.

Weekday opening times are from 10.30 a.m. till 3 p.m. and 6.30 p.m. till 11 p.m. the pub is open all day between June and September.

Telephone: (0736) 796927.

Walk No. 40

Village lies off the B3306 4½ miles south west of St. Ives.

Approx. distance of walk: 4½ miles. O.S. Map No. 203 454/385.

There is a car park just down the lane near the Folk Museum.

A quite strenuous coast path walk across some of Cornwalls most dramatic cliff scenery where the path plunges down to the shoreline and the next moment rises high onto the cliffs above. The inland return route is level across fields.

1. From the pub bear left past the church and soon turn left onto a trackway signed "Zennor Head" remaining on this to a large white house "Carn Cobba" then proceed ahead onto the coast path signed "St. Ives" and shortly reach Zennor Head with dramatic views down into Pendour Cove below and to Pendeen Lighthouse away to the left.
2. The coast path from Zennor Head is very narrow in places with some steep and often shaley ascents and descents across the cliffs. From the top of the headlands the reward of some stunning scenery makes the effort all worthwhile. The lower slopes of the shelving cliffs are home to cuckoos, finches, pipits and stonechats and in early summer honeysuckle abounds and orchids can be seen amongst the bracken. The path goes round Wicca Pool, across Mussel Point and around the headland with "The Carracks", a rock outcrop just offshore. It is also known as Seal Island as seals are regularly seen basking on the rocks.
3. Just beyond this headland the path forks, take the inland route along the edge of a valley, bear right uphill along a concrete drive and shortly enter Treveal farm. Keep left in front of the main house following the high-hedged trackway gradually uphill, bear right at a junction of tracks passing Boscubben farmhouse on the right.
4. Soon enter the farmyard at Wicca and follow the waymarked path "Zennor" to the right of the house into a field onto what is called the Tinners Way but known locally as the Coffin Path. From here the well defined path keeps to the right hand side of the field across two stiles then follows the line of telegraph poles some of which are marked with a white dot. Pass through two thickets then pass to the left of Tregethen farm, cross the driveway and keep with the telegraph poles across five fields via stone stiles to Tremedda farm. Cross the driveway and keep to the right hand edge of the next six fields then head towards the tower of Zennor church which soon comes into view. Join a track to the right of the church then shortly turn left along the lane back to the Tinners Arms.

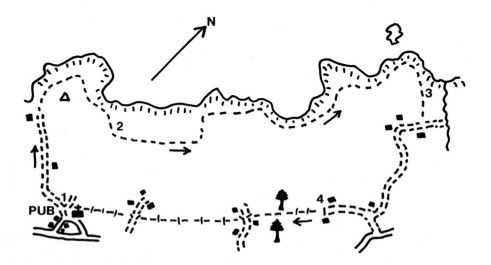